Best~dressed Children!
Easy to make clothes for 1-10 year olds

Written and designed by Jill Morris
Illustrated by Hildegarde Bone
Photography by Richard Sharpe Studios

SAMPSON LOW

Published by Sampson Low
Berkshire House, Queen Street, Maidenhead
Designed and produced for Sampson Low by
Intercontinental Book Productions
Copyright © 1974 Intercontinental Book Productions
Printed and bound in Spain by Mateu Cromo Artes Gráficas, S.A.

SBN 562 00022 4

CONTENTS

INTRODUCTION

In order to make things as easy as possible we have arranged the book as follows:

Pages 7 to 13 have all sorts of sewing instructions. There's a full list and explanation of the sewing equipment you will need, a sizing and measuring chart so that you can check the exact size of your child, (before beginning to make your patterns!), sewing instructions for stitches, sewing in zips, setting in collars and sleeves, putting up hems, and so on. Perhaps most important of all, on page 8, there are full instructions for how to use the graph patterns given with each of the sewn garments. We would strongly recommend that you read the *whole of this section very carefully before* starting on any garment in the book. It contains lots of sound useful information pertaining specifically to this book.

Following this, on pages 14–73 are the patterns for the sewn garments for children. Fresh and unique designs, they will appeal as much to fashion conscious youngsters as to their parents. Follow our step-by-step instructions for making each garment and you should have no problems. If however, this is your first sewing venture, do try one or two of the easier things first, the Mini-Pini, for example, on page 14, or for an older child, the skirts on pages 64–67. If you launch straight into the beautiful, tailored, and rather more complicated Fur Coat on page 40 without trying anything else first—you may just be a little disappointed with your results.

Remember for all garments to use suitable fabrics for the particular item you are making. For coats use coatweight fabric or your results will simply not be as pleasing. Similarly, buy zips, buttons, bias bindings, sewing threads and any trimmings such as braid, that really match your fabric beautifully.

On pages 74–79 there are instructions for how to knit and crochet, along with notes on tension, pressing, sewing-up and so on. Once again we do advise careful reading of these pages before starting on any of the lovely knitting patterns that begin on page 80 and go through to the end of the book. It is the final touches to knitted garments that can make them look professional!

In all cases the amount of material or wool and the sewing requirements such as number and size of buttons, length of zip etc. are listed under the YOU WILL NEED heading. We have not included such things as pins, needles, tacking cotton, sewing machine, scissors and so on which you will need constantly.

W.S. and R.S. are frequently referred to in our instructions. They mean Wrong Side or sides of fabric, and Right Side or sides of fabric respectively. So R.S. together means 'place the right sides of both pieces of fabric together', prior to pinning, tacking or stitching. Where we have said 'stitch' in the instructions, it indicates machine stitching. 'Sew' means hand-sewing (type of stitch is usually stipulated).

SEWING INFORMATION

Before you begin to sew check through to make sure you have all the essential sewing equipment. You will need:

Squared dressmaker's paper, Ruler, Felt-tip pen, Pencil and Sellotape—for making your paper patterns.

Pins—use the rustless kind. Glass-headed pins are particularly easy to use and show up well on most fabrics.

Needles—of various sizes so that you have fine needles for delicate fabrics, and thicker ones for woollens and so on. A packet of assorted needles should provide you with all you need. You should also have a darning needle and a crewel needle.

Sewing Thread—you will need a selection of colours and thicknesses. Mercerised cotton is particularly good. In addition you should have a reel of tacking cotton (soft and cheaper than sewing cotton), cotton thread for thicker materials and buttonhole twist for working buttonholes and loops.

Bodkin—helps in threading elastic through hemmed openings. Alternatively you can use a safety pin.

Scissors—you need an ordinary pair of scissors for cutting out your paper patterns, a medium or large sharp pair of dressmaker's scissors for cutting out fabric and a small pair of sharp pointed scissors for cutting buttonholes, clipping into curves etc.

Thimble—to fit on to the middle finger of your sewing hand.

Tape measure—those made of glass fibre with metal ends are the best as they do not stretch.

Iron and Ironing Board—keep close by and ready for use all the time you are sewing. You should be using them frequently!

Sewing Machine—most of the garments in the first section of this book were made with the use of a sewing machine. As explained on p.9 it is not possible to talk specifically about sewing machines as there are now so many different ones on the market. The important thing is to thoroughly read the handbook provided with your machine and practise all stitches extensively before using it to make garments.

There are other items of equipment that can make dressmaking a little easier, but are not absolutely essential. These include:

Tailor's Chalk, or a Tracing Wheel and Dressmaker's Carbon Paper—for transferring details from patterns on to the fabric.

Unpicking Gadget—useful for unpicking rows of machining when necessary.

A Sewing Gauge with a moveable marker—can be useful for checking the width of a hem as you turn it up.

Magnet—useful for picking up spilt pins and tidying up after a sewing session.

Pinking Shears—as they cut with a serrated edge, they can be useful for neatening the edge of some materials. Not as efficient as neatening by hand or machine stitching.

Pincushion—for pins and needles.

Sleeveboard—useful for pressing around cuffs and armholes.

MEASUREMENT CHART

Age/Size	6 months	1 year	2 years	3 years	4 years	5 years	6 years	7 years	8 years
CHEST	ins. 19	ins. 20	ins. 21	ins. 22	ins. 23	ins. 24	ins. 25	ins. 26	ins. 27
WAIST	19	19½	20	20½	21	21½	22	23	23½
HIP	—	—	—	—	24	25	26	27	28
BACK NECK LENGTH	—	8¼	8½	9	9½	10	10½	11½	12
APPROX. HEIGHT	28	31	34	37	40	43	46	50	52

HOW TO TAKE MEASUREMENTS

CHEST	Take tape measure round fullest part of the chest.
WAIST	Take tape measure round the natural waistline.
HIP	Take tape measure round fullest part of the body below waist.
BACK NECK LENGTH	Take tape measure from the prominent bone at the back neck to the waistline.

MAKING PAPER PATTERNS

All the patterns for the garments in this book are given as graph patterns, which means they must be made into paper patterns before they can be used. This is easily done by transferring them on to dressmaker's squared paper (available from haberdashery departments of large stores and fabric shops). The easiest way to make a paper pattern is as follows:

1. Check the scale on the graph pattern. Unless otherwise stated, 1 square on each of our patterns equals 3 inches, i.e. each square on our patterns equals 3 of the 1-inch squares, clearly marked on dressmaker's squared paper.

2. Number the squares on graph patterns across the top and down the sides. Number pattern paper in the same way, taping pieces together if necessary.

3. Draw all vertical and horizontal straight lines of pattern pieces first. Mark dots on lines of pattern paper to correspond with ends of curved lines on graph patterns.

4. Join up dots following curves of graph pattern. Rub out and draw again if they are not correct. Transfer all words and markings on to your pattern as well.

5. Check the pattern pieces against the child to make sure they fit and make any alterations necessary at *this* stage. Then cut out the pattern pieces. If you feel you will use the pattern again, make a trace-off duplicate pattern, using the original as the master.

6. Place and carefully pin each pattern piece on to the fabric. Our graph patterns have been designed to show the correct way to fold the material and place the pattern pieces for the most economical use of fabric, so use them as a guide. Most pattern pieces need to be cut on double fabric as 2 pieces are needed for the garment.
Note that instructions are given with the patterns for making them a size smaller or larger, and that all graph patterns include $\frac{1}{2}$ in. seam allowance.
When you have cut out the garment follow the making-up instructions, trying the garment on the child at anytime you are not sure of the fit. Pay particular attention to collars, sleeves and hemlines.
All the seams used in this book are plain or open seams, i.e. the 2 pieces of fabric placed right sides together and machined down the seam line, which is $\frac{1}{2}$ in. from the raw edges. Press all seams at each stage of making and neaten them, either by oversewing (see page 9) or by turning under a tiny single hem (i.e. just one layer of material turned over.) and machining along this.

TACKING STITCH

Tacking is used to hold 2 pieces of material together, prior to fitting or machining. It should be worked along the line where machining will take place. All garments should be tacked together and tried on and fitted before machining is commenced.
To tack, thread needle with a long piece of thread and knot one end. Make even stitches $\frac{1}{2}$ in. long parallel with the edge, through both thicknesses of fabric. Fasten end by taking 2 stitches back through the material.

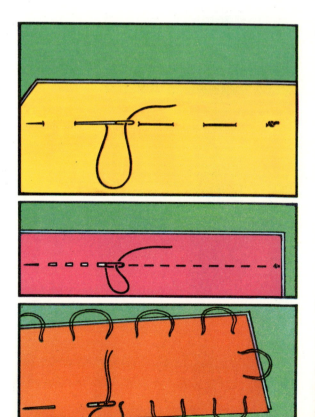

RUNNING STITCH

Running is worked in the same way as tacking except the stitches should be $\frac{1}{8}$ in. long. 4 or more stitches can be drawn away from the work. Running stitch is used when gathering is required—such as round sleeve heads or tops of skirts.

TAILOR'S TACKS

This is a quick way of marking pattern outlines or details such as darts or pleats.

1. Use a really long thread of double tacking cotton and then tack in the usual way—see Tacking Stitch—but leave each stitch quite loose so that it lies in a loop on the surface.

2. When tacking is complete, gently pull the two thicknesses apart as far as the loops will extend—usually about $\frac{1}{2}$ in. Cut the stitches apart between the two surfaces, and each will be found to be marked accurately with the short ends of thread.

You can also use tailor's chalk or a tracing wheel to mark pattern details on fabric.

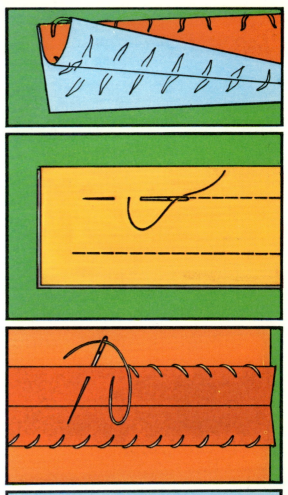

BACK STITCH

All hand sewing should begin and end with 1 or 2 back stitches in order to secure the thread. It is very firm stitching and can be used for joining fabric together instead of machining.

Thread needle and knot thread. Working from right to left, bring needle through fabric from back and put back into material $\frac{1}{8}$ in. *back* from where it came through. Bring it out $\frac{1}{8}$ in. in front. Put back into fabric at end of previous stitch and bring out a stitch length in front. Repeat along line.

OVERSEWING

This is a method of neatening a plain seam after it has been opened and pressed flat. It can also be used to join 2 edges of material together.

Starting from the underside of the fabric, working from left to right put your needle in the cloth $\frac{1}{4}$ in. from the edge. Pull through, allowing the thread to loop over the raw edge of the cloth. Repeat this but $\frac{1}{4}$ in. further along the raw edge. Continue until the raw edge is neatened.

HERRINGBONE STITCH

This is often used as a decorative stitch but can also be used to secure one piece of fabric to another firmly—but very neatly.

Work from left to right. Use two parallel lines to guide the stitches. Bring the needle through from the wrong side at one end of the upper line. Take the thread forward and downward to the lower line, then pick up a small horizontal stitch with the needle pointing backwards.

Pull through, take the needle diagonally upwards and forwards to the upper line and make another backward stitch there. (Needle should come out level with the beginning of the proceeding stitch—see diagram.) Continue stitching alternatively on the two lines, so that a kind of cross stitch is formed.

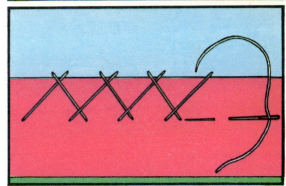

MACHINING STITCHING

Make sure you understand how to use your machine before attempting any sewing of garments. Practise all the stitches and tensions on scraps of fabric.

The instruction book of your machine will give you all the details of threads and needles. It is not possible to give them all here as manufacturers instructions vary.

Many machines have useful attachments. Learn how to use them all as most of them will save you time when stitching garments.

PUTTING UP HEMS

1. PLAIN HEM—SLIPSTITCH

This is used when the fabric is thin and the garment a simple shape with no surplus fullness at the hemline.

Fold fabric $\frac{1}{2}$ in. from the raw edge to W.S. Then make a further turning. (The size of this turning should be about 2 in.; if more has to be turned to make the garment the right depth, cut off surplus.) Pin and tack fabric in place. This is the actual hemline of the garment. Thread the needle and, at the first fold line, working from right to left, insert the needle and pull through. $\frac{1}{4}$—$\frac{1}{2}$ in. along from your first stitch insert the needle into the skirt fabric. Take up the minimum amount of material on your needle, and pull thread through. Move another $\frac{1}{4}$—$\frac{1}{2}$ in. along and insert the needle into the fold line again. Continue slip-stitching making sure the stitches are not pulled too tightly or they will show on the right side of the garment. Finish by taking a small stitch back through the material and out through the fold.

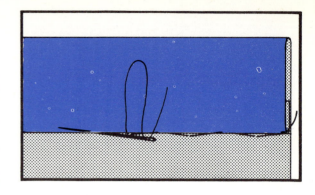

2. FLARED OR GATHERED HEM

This is used for turning up a bottom edge which is flared, bell-shaped or very definitely curved. In such cases the raw edge is distinctly wider than the part to which it is hemmed.

The fullness of the hem can be dealt with in various ways. Either run a gathering thread round hem $\frac{3}{4}$ in. from raw edge and pull up to 'fit the skirt'. The hem should be as flat as possible. Alternatively, make tiny darts, tucks or pleats at regular intervals round the hem to dispose of fullness.

When the hem fits the skirt, stitch skirt tape or binding to the edge and hem this down onto the garment. Skirt tape is a flat tape and is used to avoid the bulky line which would result from turning the raw edge of the fabric inside and hemming.

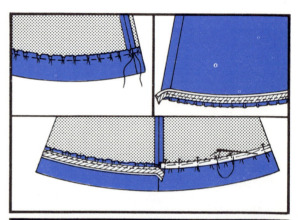

WORKING A BUTTONHOLE

When making a row of buttonholes mark each one carefully before starting. Making sure they lie directly under one another at even distances apart.

1. Mark your buttonhole in pencil or tailor's chalk.

2. Sew a small running stitch, through the two thicknesses all round the buttonhole mark. This is to stop it fraying when it is cut.

3. Cut the buttonhole.

4. Work buttonhole stitch all round the raw edges as follows:

To start make a straight upward stitch the depth required (usually $\frac{1}{8}$ in.).

Put the needle through to the wrong side at the end of this stitch bringing it up again on the raw edge of the buttonhole slit, where it originally came from.

Make a second upright stitch, this time downwards towards the raw edge, holding the thread down with the left thumb so that it is under the needle. Pull up the needle. Pull up the thread, and it will form a base along the raw edge, known as the 'purl'. Continue to take upright stitches, bringing the needle back to the raw edge each stitch touching the previous stitch. Always keep the thread under the needle. When turning a corner, make a diagonal stitch going, at its inner end, into the same hole as the last upright stitch, and take the first upright stitch on the new line also into this hole; this gives a symmetrical effect.

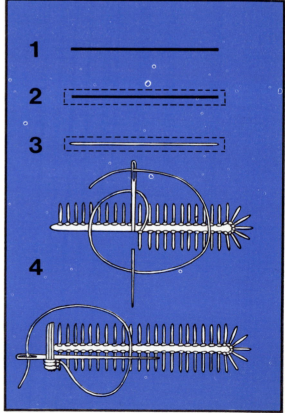

WORKED LOOPS

Used at the edges of some garments for fastening buttons. Sew 3 or 4 strands through folded edge of material leaving them loose to the depth of the intended loop. Work buttonhole stitch over all threads right round the loop.

CROSSWAY OR BIAS STRIPS

Crossway or bias strips are usually used to bind curved edges. As they are cut diagonally across the fabric, on the true bias, they can be slightly stretched, without distorting, to fit neatly round curves.

1. Cut strips of required width at 45° angle to the straight edges of fabric. Do this by folding fabric diagonally so the crosswise grain is parallel to the lengthwise grain.

2. Place 'A' and 'B', right sides together and stitch.

3. Press open and trim away points that extend over the edges. You have a straight 'stretchy' strip with a diagonal seam.
Bought bias binding is also available and is particularly useful when you have insufficient fabric to cut crossway strips.

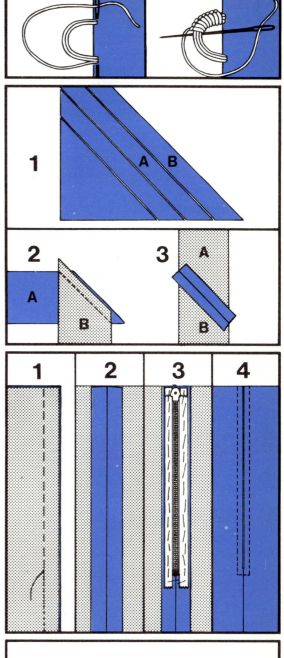

INSERTING A ZIP

1. Insert zip after you have machined the seam and neatened the edges. Right sides of fabric together, tack 2 sides of zip opening together, continuing in a straight line from the machining, and using small stitches.

2. Press open.

3. Lay zip against centre of tacked seamline, and tack into position.

4. On right side of garment machine close to the zip. (You will achieve best results by using the zipper foot, available for most sewing machines.) Remove seam tacking and your zip will remain perfectly concealed.

SETTING A COLLAR

Make up the collar by placing right sides top collar and undercollar together, (interfacing tacked to W.S. of under collar, if need) then tacking and machining together leaving the neck edge unstitched. Trim turnings and turn collar to right side. Press.
To set the collar on, mark the exact back centre of the neckline on the garment with a pin and that of the underside of the collar with another.
Match the two pins and tack from them each way to the

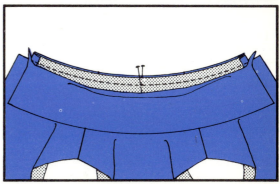

collar fronts, the under collar resting on the right side of the garment. Do not tack the upper collar. Try on the garment, make sure the collar is central. Stitch in place.

Turn under the raw edge of the top collar and slip-stitch in place over raw edges of garments' collar.

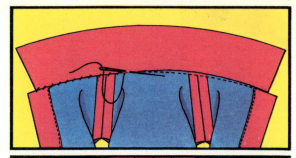

SETTING A SLEEVE

Stitch the underarm seam on the sleeve and press. Run a gathering thread round the head of the sleeve $\frac{1}{2}$ in. from the edge. Make sure you have the correct sleeve for the correct armhole.

Hold the garment with its wrong side towards you and the armhole well opened.

With the sleeve right side out, draw it through the armhole so that the edges of the sleeve and the armhole are level and you look into the wrong side of the sleeve. (Garment and sleeve are right side together.)

Match the centre of the sleeve to the shoulder seam of the garment. Pin the lower part of the sleeve and armhole together matching seams. Adjust the gathers of the upper sleeve part so that grain of the fabric hangs vertically down the sleeve. Pin the upper part to the armhole. Tack over the pins (see sketch) adjusting gathers. If it is a plain sleeve there should be a hardly noticeable fullness. Remove the pins and try the garment on the child. If it is comfortable and hangs well stitch it in. If not, adjust, pin and re-tack.

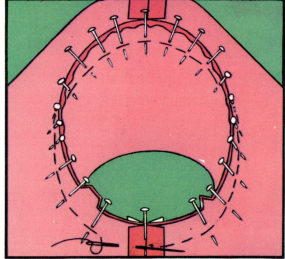

DARTS

Some of the patterns in this book have darts incorporated in them, which help in shaping the garment. To work these, mark the lines of the dart from the pattern using tailor's tacks, chalk or a tracing wheel. Fold fabric along centre of dart, R.S. inside and pin and tack in place. Machine stitch from the widest end towards the fold, so that the last few stitches come on the fold. Press the dart flat and then press it to one side.

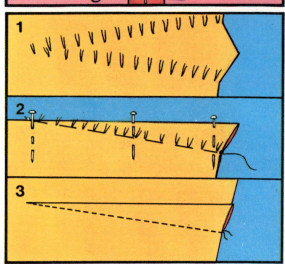

FACINGS

Raw edges must always be neatened when making garments and 'facings' are often used in such places as neck, sleeve, front opening and pocket edges. Facings are usually cut as a separate pattern piece and have been clearly shown on the graph patterns. Instructions for applying them are given in the individual making-up instructions.

Curved edges on garments such as round sleeves, necklines, trouser crutch seams etc. must be 'clipped' so they lie flat. To do this take small snips at approximate $\frac{1}{2}$–1 in. intervals from the edge of the fabric down to the machined seam line. Press seam flat.

SMOCKING

The preliminary gathering of smocking is extremely important to the finished appearance—so it should be carefully and unhurriedly done. The dots can be marked at $\frac{1}{2}$ in. or less intervals and on 2 to 4 times the required finished width of the smocking. Because of the concentration of the fabric, it is usually done on lightweight fabric.

1. Lay the material flat and pin, or tack it to tissue paper so that it does not move when you start marking it.

2. Using a ruler mark every $\frac{1}{2}$ in. along and each row 1 in. apart with a pencil.

3. Tack, taking the needle in and out of consecutive dots. Make sure stitches fall directly under each other in all lines.

4. When you have completed all rows, draw up the gathers and arrange them evenly. You can use a pin at the end of each row to secure the surplus thread. The gathered measurement should be one-third of the original length.

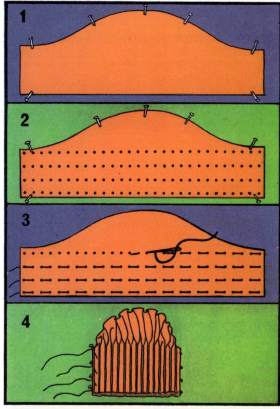

There are many embroidery stitches suitable for smocking, most of which are quite simple to do and look extremely attractive. The one used on the Long Party Dress on page 68 is called 'Honeycomb' and we give instructions for it on this page.

1. Thread the needle with embroidery thread and bring through the fabric from the wrong side at the left pleat of the second row.

2. Sew a back stitch which catches together the next pleat to the first one, in the same row, and the first one itself.

3. Sew another back stitch below the first one and then insert the needle into the second of the two pleats. Carry the needle up inside the pleat, so that it does not show, to the row immediately above.

4. As before back stitch this pleat to the next. (this is the third pleat from the left as the stitch was started on the second).

5. This time put the needle downwards inside the third pleat, taking it down to the lower row. Continue in this way back-stitching together two pleats alternately in the lower and upper rows, the second pleat in one stitch always becoming the first in the next, so that a diamond pattern is formed.

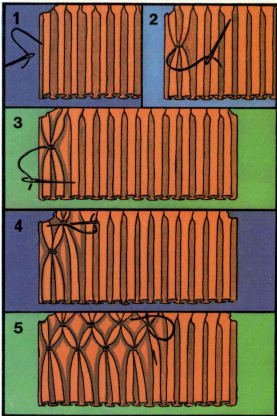

Mini-Pini Cover-Up

This pretty little smock cover-up could be made in towelling or PVC and so double as a bib. We chose crisp broderie anglaise —and the little dress worn underneath was made using the pattern for a christening gown on the next page.

TO ADJUST YOUR PATTERN:
Pattern is Size 1.
For one size larger lengthen by 1 in.
For a smaller size reduce by 1 in.

YOU WILL NEED:
$\frac{1}{2}$ yd 34 in./35 in. wide broderie anglaise
Matching sewing thread
$2\frac{1}{2}$ yds edging lace

1

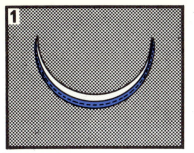

Cut out shapes shown for the armholes. Neaten the underarm (i.e. lower half of crescent shape).

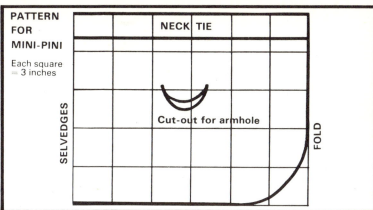

PATTERN FOR MINI-PINI

Each square = 3 inches

NECK TIE

SELVEDGES

Cut-out for armhole

FOLD

2

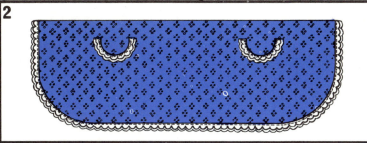

Gather lace to fit top armhole crescent shape and stitch in place. Press seam towards neck, and stitch round the curve. Run a gathering thread round lace, pull up and sew round the hem, pressing and top stitching in the same way.

3

Run a gathering thread round neck edge and pull up to required size—(measure child's neck and add $1\frac{1}{2}$ in.)

4

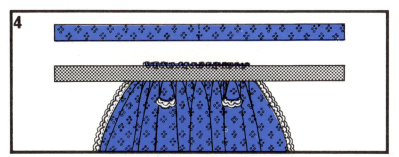

Divide neck tie in half. Place RS centre front of neck tie to RS centre front of cover-up. Pin one side of neck tie to neck edge adjusting gathers evenly. Pin other side.

5

Tack into position. Then fold in raw edges of the remainder of ties either side of the neck. Tack.

6

Fold over to cover raw edge of the binding on the neck. Tack. Stitch carefully through the whole length of the neck tie. Press.

Christening Gown

This enchanting pattern for a christening gown is for a six-month old baby. Enlarge the pattern as instructed overleaf to make a child's dress for a one year old baby.

YOU WILL NEED:
$1\frac{1}{3}$ yds 34 in./35 in. wide Broderie Anglaise flouncing.
Matching Sewing Thread
Shirring elastic
Broderie Anglaise trim: approx 4 yds double-edged with ribbon slotting: approx $\frac{1}{2}$ yd edging
4 yds narrow satin ribbon
12 make-up satin ribbon bows
$3\frac{3}{8}$ in. buttons, or smaller if preferred.

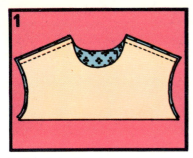

1 R.S. of body pieces together, pin, tack and stitch shoulder seams.

2 R.S. of skirt pieces together, pin, tack and stitch side seams.

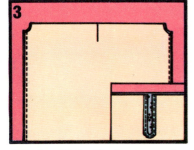

3 Cut the slit for the back opening in the skirt. Turn edges to W.S. and slip stitch to neaten.

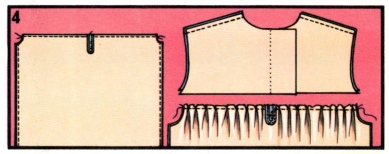

4 Run a gathering thread around top of skirt and draw up to fit bodice. Bodice back has an allowance for buttons and button-holes, so turn back on the marked line.

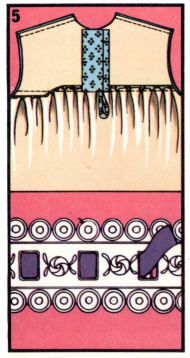

5 R.S. together, tack and stitch skirt to bodice overlapping centre of back bodice yoke. Thread satin ribbon through lace.

6 Sew lace on to dress. Positions for the double-edged lace are: Approx. $\frac{1}{3}$ of skirt length down from bodice yoke seam; halfway between this and the hem; over the bodice/skirt seam (only a small amount should cover the skirt).

17

7

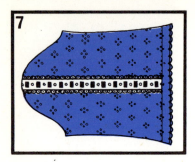

Stitch lace down centre of sleeves to the wrist, stopping at elastication level.

8

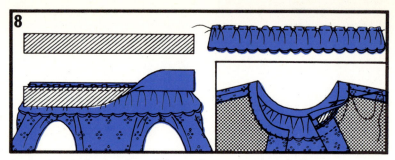

Gather broderie anglaise edging and sew round neck. Cut a cross-way strip $1\frac{1}{4}$ in. × $10\frac{1}{2}$ in. and stitch to R.S. neck edge. Turn over to cover the raw edges and slip stitch into position.

9

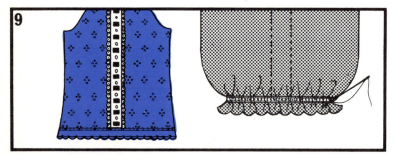

Wind shirring elastic onto the bobbin of your machine following machine manufacturer's instructions. Stitch two rows $\frac{1}{4}$ in. apart along marked lines at wrist level on sleeves. Tie the ends of shirring elastic very securely.

10

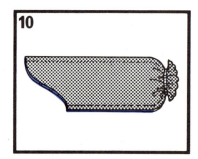

R.S. inside , tack and stitch sleeve seam.

11

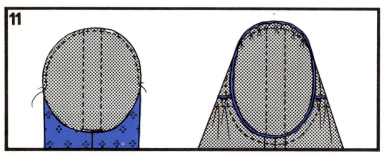

Using running stitch, sew gathering thread round sleeve head and draw up to fit armhole. With R.S. of sleeve to R.S. garment, pin, tack and stitch in place (see page 12).

12

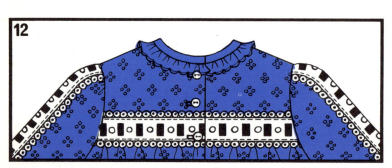

Make machine or hand-worked buttonholes at back yoke of garment. (see page 10). Sew on buttons.

13

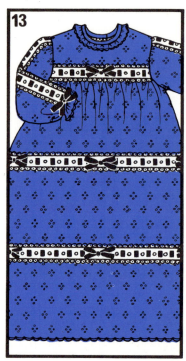

With small slip stitches, sew the made-up satin ribbon bows on to the gown.

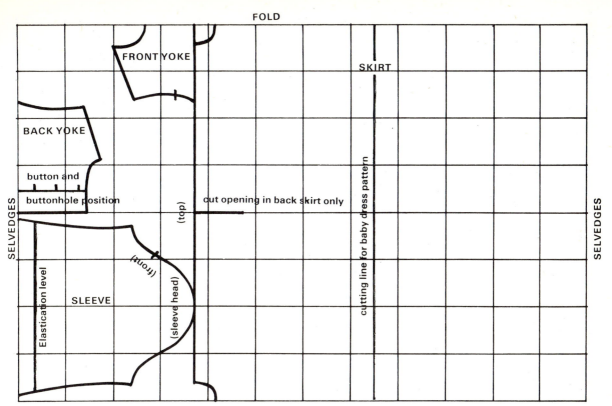

PATTERN FOR CHRISTENING GOWN

Each square = 3 inches

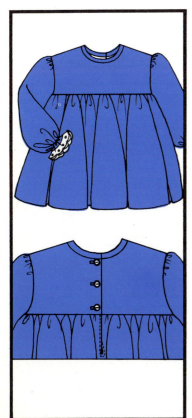

TO ADJUST YOUR PATTERN:

To adapt the christening gown to ake a size one baby dress shown at left, follow the enlarging instructions given on page 16. Cut the skirt below along the dotted line shown on the pattern.

To make baby dress pattern for size one you should make the following adjustments to your pattern:

FRONT YOKE: Extend yoke width by $\frac{1}{4}$ in.
Raise shoulder seam by $\frac{1}{4}$ in.

BACK YOKE: As front yoke.

SLEEVE: Raise top point of sleeve by $\frac{1}{4}$ in. Extend width of sleeve at underarm point by $\frac{1}{4}$ in. Redraw sleeve head connecting the new measurements. Lengthen bottom of sleeve by $1\frac{1}{8}$ in.

FRONT SKIRT: Extend skirt width by $\frac{1}{4}$ in.
Lengthen skirt 1 in.

BACK SKIRT: As front skirt.

For size two, extend your size one pattern by the same adjustments as above. To make up the garment as a baby dress, follow the instructions for making up the christening gown, but *omit* the double-edged lace application instructions on the sleeves and skirt. Add narrow lace edging to sleeves at the wrists.

The hem allowance on the pattern is $1\frac{1}{2}$ in.

Dungarees

Make up these dungarees in plain material as we have and put on a motif, or use the same pattern and make up the dungarees in check, striped or any printed material.

TO ADJUST YOUR PATTERN:
The pattern is in Size 2.
Seam allowance is $\frac{1}{2}$ in.
Hem allowance on legs $1\frac{1}{4}$ in.
Back waist casing for elastic $1\frac{1}{4}$ in.

To make the pattern a size larger, adjust as follows:
FRONT: Keeping crutch point the same, extend length at top by $1\frac{1}{4}$ in. Widen by $\frac{1}{8}$ in. Extend length upwards at side seam by $\frac{1}{2}$ in. Re-draw chest area connecting the new measurements. Widen dungaree at crutch level inside leg by $\frac{1}{4}$ in. Lengthen dungaree legs by 2 in.
BACK: Keeping crutch point the same, extend length at top by $\frac{1}{2}$ in. Widen dungarees at crutch level inside leg by $\frac{1}{4}$ in. Lengthen dungarees by 2 in.
STRAPS: Lengthen to desired measurement.
For a size smaller make similar adjustments but as reductions.

YOU WILL NEED:
$1\frac{1}{2}$ yds 36 in. wide material.
Matching Sewing thread.
Buttonhole Twist.
2 $\frac{3}{4}$ in. buttons.
Scraps of White, Orange, Green and Red fabric for motif
Small amount of black and white material for the rabbit's trousers
Embroidery thread.
Elastic $\frac{1}{2}$ in. wide.

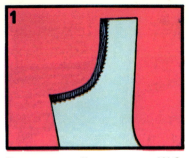

1 Turn seam allowance to W.S. on arm curve of dungarees front. Machine or slipstitch into position.

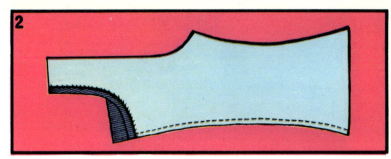

2 R.S. front and back pieces together, stitch side seams, machining from hem, upwards. The surplus material at the top of the dungaree back will be folded over later.

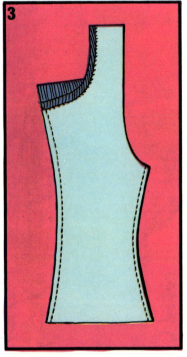

3 R.S. together, pin, tack and stitch front leg to back leg at inside leg seams.

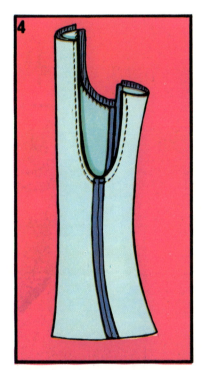

4 Place one leg inside other with R.S. together. Pin, matching inside leg seams at crutch. Tack and stitch. Clip curved seams.

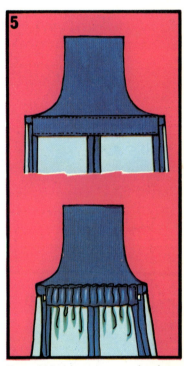

5 Turn $1\frac{1}{2}$ in. hem at top back to W.S. Slip stitch. Thread elastic through. Stitch one end; adjust to child's size and sew down end.

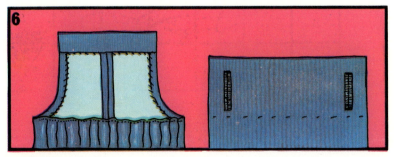

6 Turn seam allowance of $1\frac{1}{4}$ in. on front piece to W.S. for the top of the dungaree. Work buttonholes at each corner, either by machine or hand.

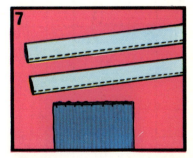

7 R.S. inside, stitch down length of straps. Turning through to R.S. Press. Turn in raw edges at ends and slip-stitch along openings.

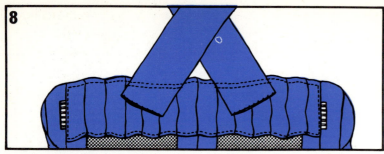

8

Sew straps to back of dungarees, at an angle to allow them to cross at the centre of the child's back. Turn under the excess material at end of straps as shown above, and slip stitch to W.S. top of dungarees to neaten.

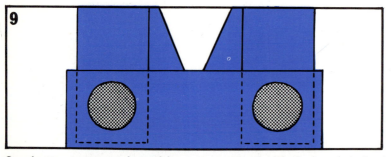

9

Sew buttons on straps in position to correspond with the buttonholes, giving sufficient length of strap to allow the child to move comfortably.

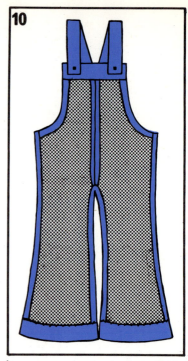

10

Turn up trouser leg hems to W.S. to fit child. Slip-stitch into position.

PATTERN FOR DUNGAREES   Each square = 3 inches

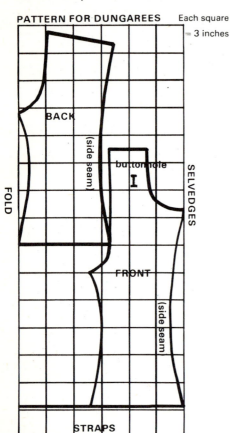

BACK

(side seam)

buttonhole

SELVEDGES

FOLD

FRONT

(side seam)

STRAPS

PATTERN FOR MOTIF   NB — each square = 2 in.

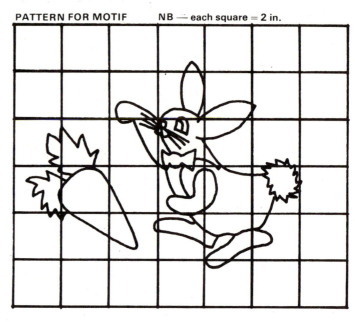

1 Motif: Cut out rabbit completely in white fabric.

2 Cut out trousers in black and white check, turn under raw edges and slip-stitch to rabbit shape.

3 Outline eyes, nose and teeth in embroidery thread. Sew whiskers. Fill in eyes with small stitches.

4 Cut out red bow tie; turn raw edges under and slip stitch to rabbit.

5 Turn raw edges round rabbit under and slip stitch in required position on right-hand side of dungarees.

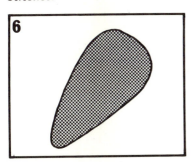

6 Cut out carrot shape from orange fabric.

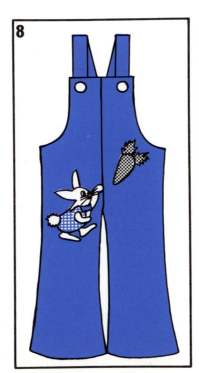

8 Turn under raw edges of both shapes. Slip stitch to dungarees so that carrot slightly overlaps carrot top.

7 Cut out carrot-top shape from green fabric.

Shorts and a Jerkin

Make up these shorts in denim or imitation suede as we have done. The jerkin is in real suede and makes a neat top for an older brother. Follow the instructions to make it smaller, so it teams up with the shorts.

TO ADJUST YOUR PATTERN:
Shorts
The pattern is in Size 4.
To make the pattern a size larger adjust as follows:
FRONT: Add $\frac{1}{2}$ in. to top of shorts. Add $\frac{1}{8}$ in. to all other seams.
BACK: Make similar adjustments as front.
POCKETS AND POCKET FACINGS: Add $\frac{1}{8}$ in. to all seams.
For a size smaller make similar adjustments but as reductions.

Suede Jerkin
The pattern is Size 6.
For a size smaller make the following adjustments.
SHOULDER SEAM: Decrease length by $\frac{1}{8}$ in.
ARMHOLE: Fill in $\frac{1}{2}$ in. at underarm level, so armhole is smaller.
WIDTH: Decrease by 1 in.
LENGTH: Decrease by 1 in.
For a size larger, make similar adjustments but as enlargements.

YOU WILL NEED:
For the Shorts:
$\frac{1}{2}$ yd of 36 in. wide fabric
Matching sewing thread
$\frac{1}{2}$ in. wide elastic
Purchased braces
Buttons (optional)

For the Jerkin:
1 suede skin 30 in. long
Matching sewing thread
Suede strips for thonging
Leather hole punch

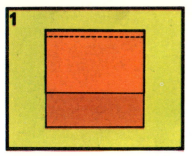

Denim shorts:
Place W.S. of pocket facing to R.S. of pocket and stitch seam. (Reverse side of fabric is used as a trim.)

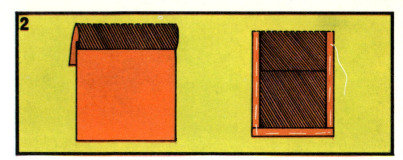

Turn top of facing under on fold line. Turn $\frac{1}{2}$ in. of raw edges of pocket to W.S. and tack.

Machine stitch diagonal lines from corners on pocket, beneath facing trim.

Pin, tack and stitch pockets to R.S. back of shorts in required positions.

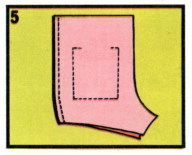

With R.S. together pin, tack and stitch side seams.

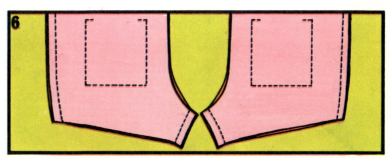

R.S. together pin, tack and stitch front leg of shorts to back leg of shorts at inside leg seam.

Place one leg inside other with R.S. together. Pin, matching inside leg seams at crutch. Tack and stitch from front to back.

Clip seams at curves so they lie flat. Turn up 1 in. to W.S. on legs, hem and slip stitch into position.

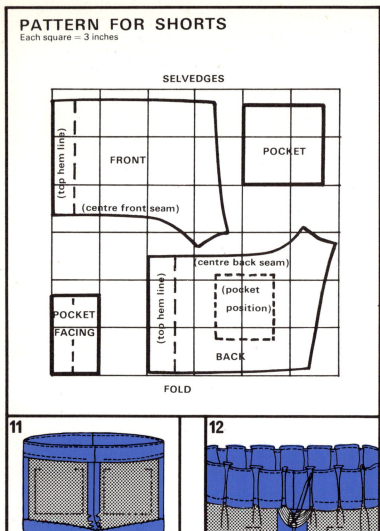

PATTERN FOR SHORTS
Each square = 3 inches

SELVEDGES

(top hem line)

FRONT

POCKET

(centre front seam)

(centre back seam)

POCKET FACING

(top hem line)

(pocket position)

BACK

FOLD

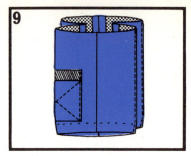

9 Fold on front crease line and top stitch a row of machining along crease.

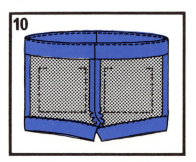

10 Turn $1\frac{1}{2}$ in. at top of shorts to W.S. and top stitch a row of machining at outer edge.

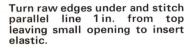

11 Turn raw edges under and stitch parallel line 1 in. from top leaving small opening to insert elastic.

12 Insert elastic and adjust to required waist size. Sew ends together securely by hand. Slip stitch opening.

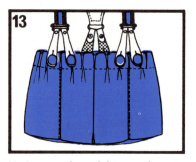

13 If the purchased braces button on to the shorts, sew buttons in required positions.

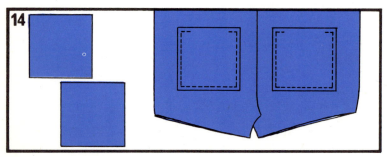

14 SUEDE SHORTS: Pocket facings are not required and it is not necessary to turn under raw edges as suede does not fray. Place pockets in required position on back of shorts and stitch without turning under edges.

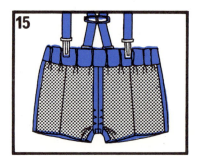

15 Proceed as for denim shorts. [There is no need to turn up and hem bottom edge, but this can be done to give a finished look.]

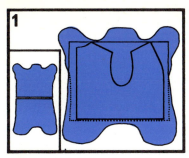

1

SUEDE JERKIN: Carefully cut suede skin in half and lay out as shown. Cut out pattern pieces using sharp scissors.

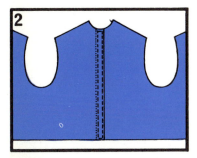

2

Overlap one back seam over other and stitch two rows.

PATTERN FOR SUEDE JERKIN

Each square = 3 inches

(centre back)

(front edge)

CUT THE SUEDE SKIN IN HALF AND PLACE RIGHT SIDES TOGETHER, MAKING SURE THE GRAIN IS RUNNING THE SAME WAY ON EACH SKIN.

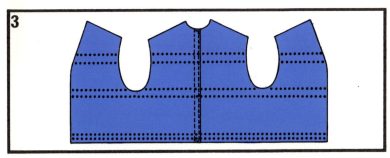

3

Punch holes $\frac{1}{2}$ in. apart at approximately these measurements *up* from the bottom. *1st Row:* $\frac{1}{2}$ in. *2nd Row:* 1 in. *3rd Row:* $5\frac{1}{2}$ in. *4th Row:* $6\frac{1}{2}$ in. *5th Row:* $9\frac{1}{2}$ in. *6th Row:* $10\frac{1}{2}$ in. 1st, 3rd and 5th rows are for thonging, the others for decoration only.

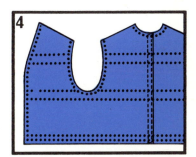

4

Punch holes $\frac{1}{2}$ in. from edge and $\frac{1}{2}$ in. apart round neck, fronts and armholes, omitting shoulder seams.

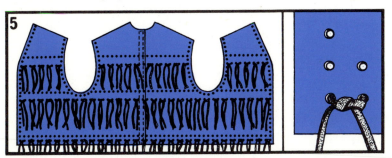

5

Cut thonging into 9 in. lengths. Thread through one hole and out through next. Tie a double knot. Repeat on 'thonging rows'.

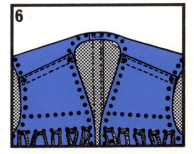

6

Overlap front shoulder onto back shoulders. Sew two rows of stitching.

Play Pinafore and Blouse

This bright little pinafore dress is very easy to make as it involves no machining—all seams are glued together. The peasant blouse is easy to make too and can be worn just as effectively with trousers or skirts.

TO ADJUST YOUR PATTERNS:
Pinafore
The pattern is in size 4.
No hem allowance as felt does not fray.
To make the pattern a size larger adjust as follows:
FRONT: Extend from neck edge, shoulder seam and armhole lines by $\frac{1}{4}$ in.
Widen side seams by $\frac{1}{4}$ in.
Place centre front $\frac{1}{8}$ in. from fold.
Lengthen pinafore by 2 in.
BACK: As for front.
For a size smaller make similar adjustments but as reductions.

YOU WILL NEED:
For the pinafore:
$\frac{3}{4}$ yd 36 in. wide felt
Matching Sewing Thread
Glue (Copydex is best)
Assorted scraps of felt in bright colours
Buttons
Thick wool for stitching
Braid to trim.

For the blouse:
1 yd 36 in. wide fabric
Matching thread
$\frac{1}{4}$ in. wide elastic
6 press-studs.

1 Fold a 5 in. square of paper as in diagram and draw the shape shown.

2 Cut out shape. Open paper fully and draw round shape on felt to make large flowers. Cut out. Glue in position on pinafore front.

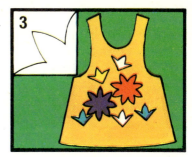

3 Refold shape and use as pattern piece for smaller flowers. Cut out 5 shapes and glue to pinafore.

4 Cut out 2 in. circles for centre of flowers. Glue to flowers and sew buttons round.

5 Using thick wool, sew large back stitches for 'stems'. Cut out small leaf shapes and glue to pinafore. One end of the leaf should touch the 'stems'.

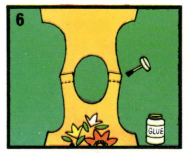

6 Take the front pinafore and overlap the back pinafore at shoulder seams by 1 in. Glue.

7 Do the same to the side seams.

8 Pin the braid trim $\frac{3}{8}$ in. in from the edges. Sew into position with running or slip stitch.

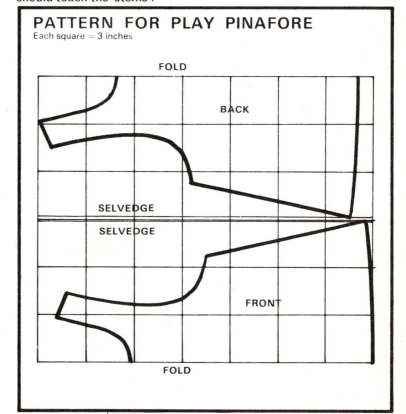

PATTERN FOR PLAY PINAFORE
Each square = 3 inches

FOLD

BACK

SELVEDGE

SELVEDGE

FRONT

FOLD

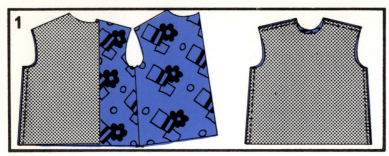

PEASANT BLOUSE: R.S. together, pin, tack and stitch shoulder and side seams together.

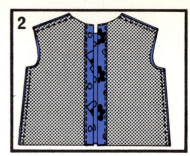

Turn centre back turning to W.S. on fold line (not centre back line). Stitch down.

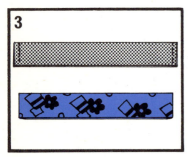

R.S. inside fold neckband lengthwise. Stitch short ends. Turn to right side out.

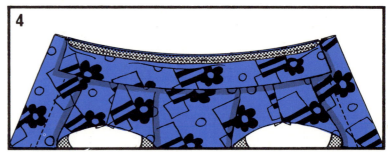

R.S. together, pin tack and stitch one edge to blouse neck from centre back round to centre back.

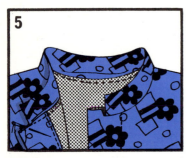

Fold in small remaining part of turning at back and slip stitch at top.

Turn neckband edge under to cover raw edges at neck and slip stitch in place.

Turn up a $\frac{1}{2}$ in. hem round bottom of blouse and stitch in place.

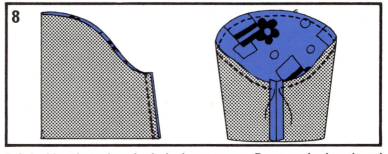

R.S. inside, pin tack and stitch sleeve seams. Run a gathering thread round each sleeve head.

PATTERN FOR BLOUSE-TOP

Each square = 3 inches

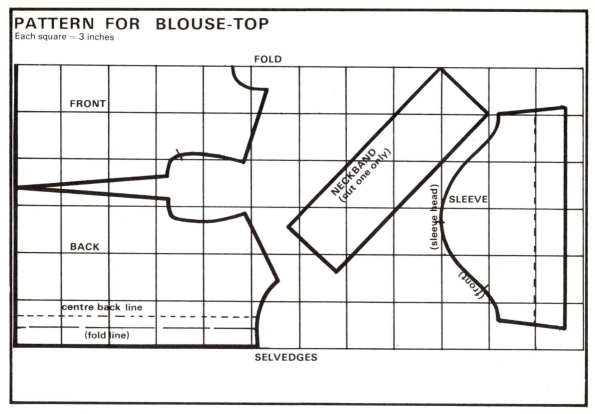

FOLD

FRONT

NECKBAND (cut one only)

SLEEVE

(sleeve head)

(front)

BACK

centre back line

(fold line)

SELVEDGES

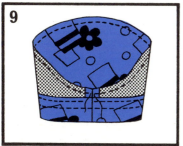

9 Turn bottom of sleeves to W.S. on fold line. Machine 2 rows $\frac{1}{2}$ in. apart 1 in. in from fold. Leave small opening.

10 Measure round child's upper arm and cut elastic 1 in. shorter. Thread through stitching round sleeve and sew ends together.

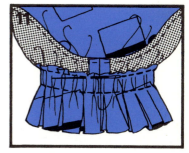

Sew opening where elastic was threaded.

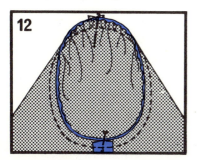

12 R.S. together, pin, tack and stitch sleeves to blouse adjusting gathers evenly round sleeve head.

13 Overlap right hand back on left. Sew 6 press-studs on W.S. of right back and R.S. of left back to fasten blouse.

A Dress or a Smock

These super little dresses are both made from the same pattern.
Make the smock from woollen material and it could team up
with a polo neck jumper on chilly days.

TO ADJUST YOUR PATTERN
The pattern is in Size 4.
To make a size larger adjust the pattern as follows:
FRONT: Widen pattern at armhole by $\frac{1}{4}$ in.
          Widen pattern at side seam by $\frac{1}{2}$ in.
          Adjust neck to required size.
          Lengthen skirt 2 in.
BACK: As for front.
SLEEVE: Widen sleeve by $\frac{1}{4}$ in. either side.
          Lengthen sleeve 1 in.
For a size smaller make similar adjustments but as reductions.

YOU WILL NEED:
for long sleeve dress:
$2\frac{1}{2}$ yds 36 in. wide fabric
Matching thread
Woven or neatened edge
   lace trimming
Buttons
Shirring elastic

for smock:
$1\frac{3}{4}$ yds 36 in. wide fabric
Matching thread
Woven or neatened edge
lace trimming
Buttons.

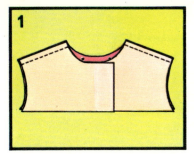

1

R.S. together, pin, tack and stitch shoulder seams of yokes.

2

Run a gathering thread round back skirt. Pull up. R.S. together pin, tack and stitch back skirt to back yoke.

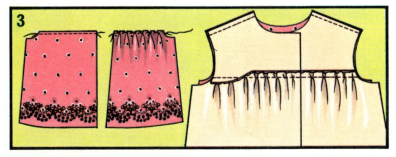

3

Run a gathering thread round front skirts. Pull up and R.S. together, pin, tack and stitch to front yokes.

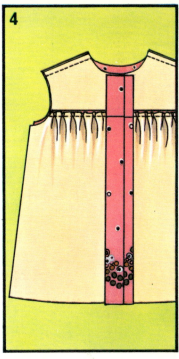

4

Fold fabric to W.S. along line at front for button and buttonhole allowance.

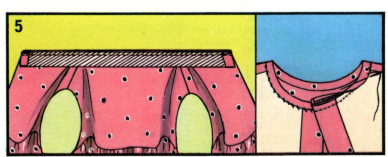

5

Pin and tack a crossway strip $12\frac{1}{2}$ in. × $1\frac{1}{2}$ in. round the neck. Stitch along one edge. Turn over to inside and slip stitch to cover raw edges.

6

R.S. together, pin, tack and stitch side seams.

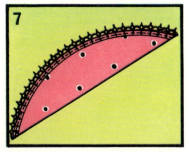

7

Turn under a small hem round bottom of sleeve frills. Stitch lace trimming to R.S. of sleeve close to edge.

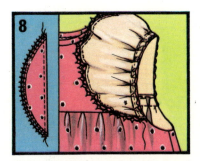

8

Run a gathering thread round top of sleeve frills. R.S. together, tack into armhole. (Sleeve frills stop at yoke level.)

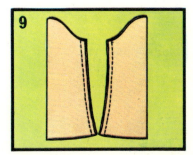

9

R.S. inside, pin, tack and stitch sleeve seam.

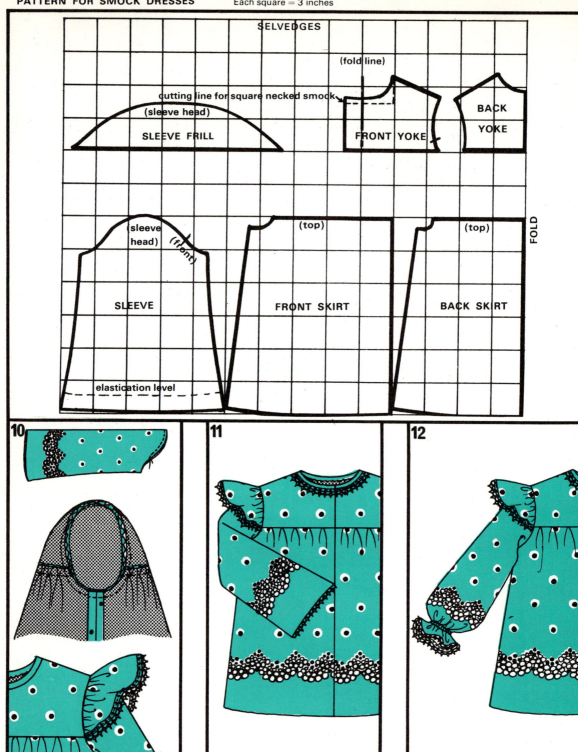

SELVEDGES

(fold line)

cutting line for square necked smock
(sleeve head)

SLEEVE FRILL

FRONT YOKE

BACK YOKE

(sleeve head) (front)

(top)

(top)

FOLD

SLEEVE

FRONT SKIRT

BACK SKIRT

elastication level

10 Gather sleeve head. R.S. together, tack into armhole. Stitch through sleeve and sleeve frill round armhole.

11 Stitch lace round sleeve hem and round neck.

12 Thread machine with shirring elastic and machine 2 rows round cuffs.

13 Turn up hem round bottom to fit child and slipstitch into position.

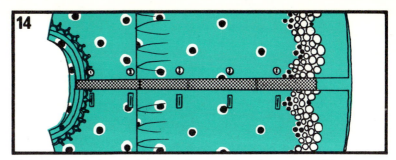

14 Make buttonholes by hand or by machine (see page 10). Sew on buttons, to correspond with these.

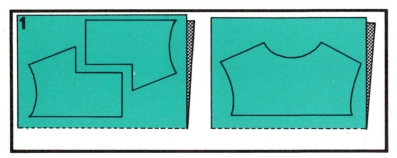

1 SMOCK: Cut along dotted lines on yoke patterns to make square neck for smocks. Cut out the yoke fronts and back on double fabric.

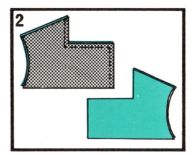

2 R.S. together, stitch round neck. Clip into corners (so neck is square and lies flat). Turn to R.S. and press.

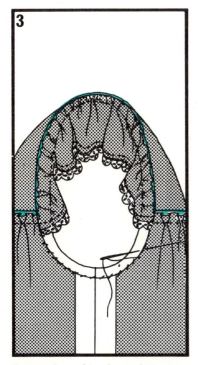

3 Proceed as for dress but turn under and slip stitch small hems on lower armholes. (Necessary as sleeves are omitted).

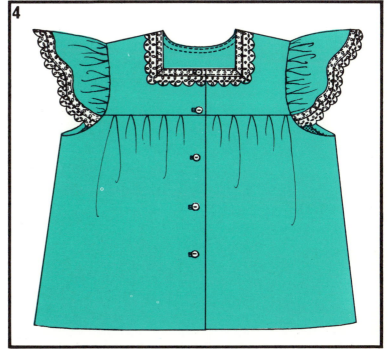

4 Trim with lace as shown.

A Coat for Indoors or Out

This smart little outdoor coat can be lengthened and made into a warm woolly housecoat.

TO ADJUST YOUR PATTERN:
Pull-on-Coat
The pattern is in size 4.
To make the pattern a size larger adjust as follows:

FRONT:	Widen pattern at armholes by $\frac{1}{4}$ in.
	Widen pattern at side seam by $\frac{1}{4}$ in.
	Lengthen coat by 2 in.
BACK:	As for front.
SLEEVE:	Widen sleeves by $\frac{1}{4}$ in. at either side at underarm seam.
	Lengthen sleeves by 1 in.
BUTTON STRAP:	Increase width by $\frac{1}{8}$ in. and lengthen by 1 in.
POCKETS:	Increase by $\frac{1}{8}$ in. all round.

For a size smaller make the same adjustments but as reductions.

YOU WILL NEED:
for coat:
$1\frac{1}{4}$ yds 54 in. wide material
Matching sewing thread
3 $\frac{3}{4}$ in. buttons
Purchased knitted ribbing

for housecoat:
2 yds 54 in. wide material
Matching sewing thread
Contrasting trim braid
Purchased knitted ribbing

PULL-ON-COAT: R.S. together, pin, tack and stitch side seams.

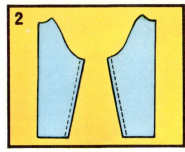

R.S. inside, pin, tack and stitch sleeve seams.

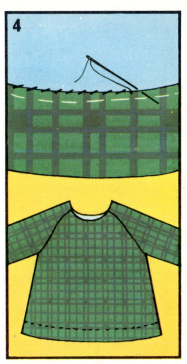

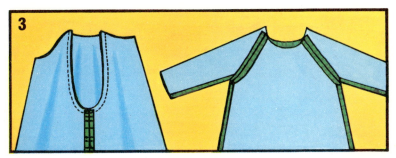

With sleeve seam matching underarm seam, R.S. together, pin, tack and stitch sleeves into coat.

Turn up hem on coat to fit child and slip stitch into position.

Turn ½ in. to W.S. all round button strap, and tack in place. Tack and slip stitch strap in position in centre of coat.

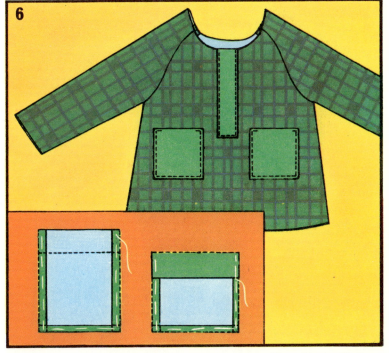

Pockets—turn to W.S. on fold line at top. Press. Turn ½ in. to W.S. on all remaining raw edges. Pin, tack and stitch into position.

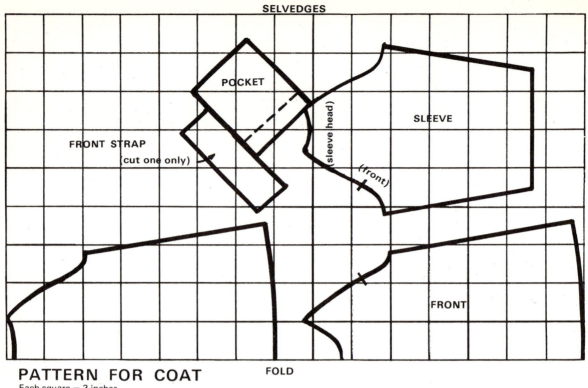

PATTERN FOR COAT
Each square = 3 inches

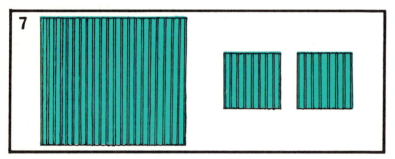

7 Cut purchased ribbing into one piece 13 in. × 11 in. for the neck and two pieces 4 in. × 4 in. for the cuffs.

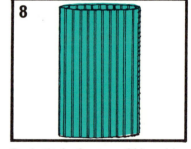

8 Backstitch the two 11 in. sides together to make a tube and turn so stitching is on inside.

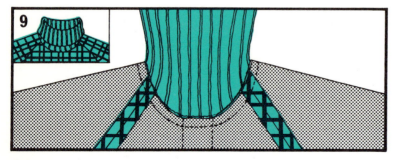

9 R.S. together sew one end to raw neck edge of coat. Fold over free end to make collar.

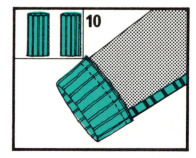

10 Sew cuff ribs into a tube in the same way. Fold and stitch raw edge to R.S. of coat at cuff edge.

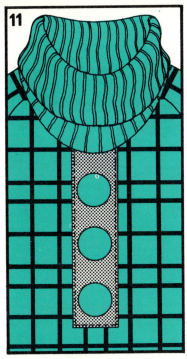

11 Sew buttons in position on button strap.

1 HOUSECOAT: Increase length of pattern to fit child's full length. Cut out pieces, omitting button strap and 1 pocket.

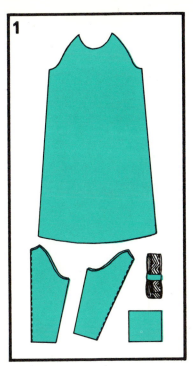

2 Make up as for coat. Stitch patterned braid down front instead of button strap.

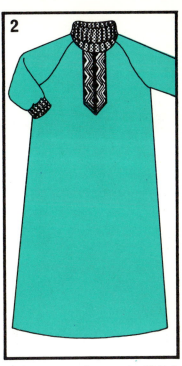

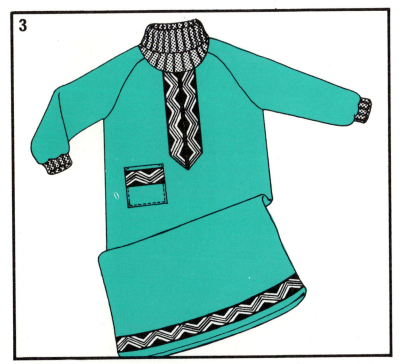

3 Attach one pocket only in the same way as coat. Stitch braid in place on top of pocket and round hem.

Fun Fur Coat and Hat

Make this luxurious coat for your child in any fur fabric. We chose ocelot for ours but others would be just as effective. The saucy little hat completes a perfect outfit.

TO ADJUST YOUR PATTERN:
The pattern is in Size 5.
To make the pattern a size larger:

BACK: Increase neck length by $\frac{1}{16}$ in. (in total). Increase shoulder seam length by $\frac{1}{8}$ in. Increase side seam width by $\frac{1}{8}$ in. Increase coat length by 2 in. Re-draw the armhole.

FRONT: Increase neck length by $\frac{1}{16}$ in. (in total). Increase shoulder seam length by $\frac{1}{8}$ in. Increase side seam width by $\frac{3}{8}$ in. Increase coat length by 2 in. Re-draw the armhole.

SLEEVES: UPPER SLEEVE: Widen sleeve by $\frac{1}{8}$ in. either side. Lengthen sleeve by $\frac{3}{4}$ in. Re-draw sleeve head. UNDER SLEEVE: Widen sleeve by $\frac{1}{16}$ in. either side. Lengthen sleeve by $\frac{3}{4}$ in. Re-draw underarm seam line.

COLLAR: Increase neck seam length by $\frac{1}{8}$ in. in total. Increase width of collar by $\frac{1}{16}$ in.

FACINGS: Re-draw front and back facings and interfacings to fit your new pattern.

For coat size 4, decrease by corresponding amount.

YOU WILL NEED:
for coat:
$1\frac{1}{2}$ yds 48 in. wide fur material
$1\frac{1}{2}$ yds 36 in. wide lining material
$\frac{1}{3}$ yd of interfacing
Matching sewing thread
Buttonhole twist
Seam binding (optional)
Small button for neck
3 $\frac{3}{4}$ in. buttons

for hat:
$\frac{1}{2}$ yd. 48 in. wide fur material
Matching sewing thread
Petersham ribbon
Elastic

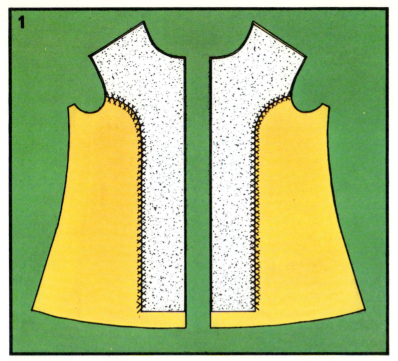

1 Pin interfacing to W.S. of coat fronts. Attach curved edge of interfacing to coat body by herring-bone stitch.

2 Pin, tack and stitch lining pockets to R.S. of coat fronts and coat back, matching notches.

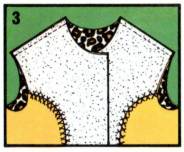

3 R.S. back and fronts together, pin, tack and stitch shoulder seams.

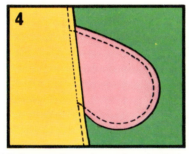

4 R.S. together, pin, tack and stitch side seams, starting at underarm, continuing round pocket and down to hem.

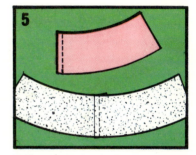

5 R.S. together, stitch centre seam of under collar. Stitch interfacing collar but overlap seam allowance at centre back.

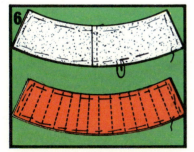

6 Place interfacing on to W.S. of under-collar. Tack round edge. Stitch rows $\frac{1}{2}$ in. apart, top to bottom, right across collar.

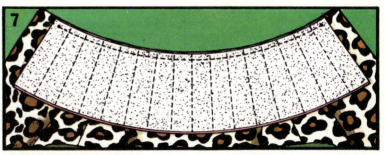

7 Pin R.S. of lining under-collar to R.S. of coat fabric at neck edge. Tack and stitch between dots.

Each square = 3 inches

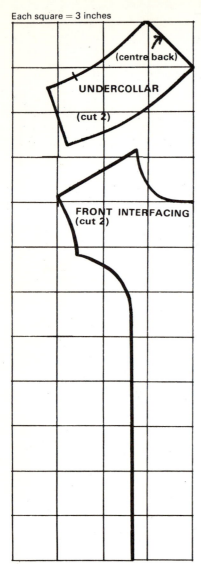

PATTERN FOR INTERFACING

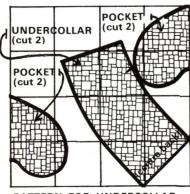

PATTERN FOR UNDERCOLLAR
AND POCKETS IN LINING

Each square = 3 inches

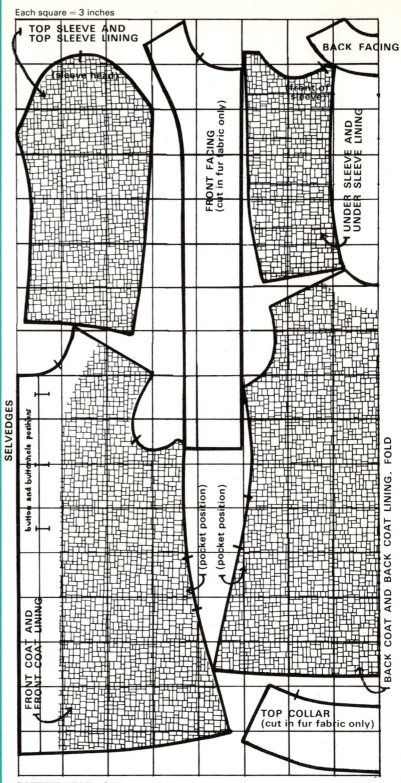

PATTERN FOR COAT

NB shaded area=pattern pieces to be cut in lining
material also.

42

8 R.S. together, pin, tack and stitch back neck facing to front neck facings.

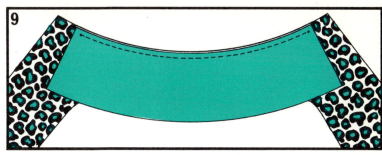

9 R.S. together, pin upper collar to facing. Tack and stitch between dots. (At this stage, coat is quite separate from facings and upper collar.)

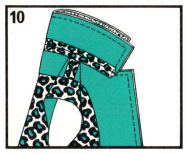

10 R.S. together, pin upper collar and facing to coat and under-collar. Tack, easing upper collar to fit. Stitch.

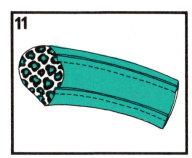

11 R.S. together, pin, tack and stitch undersleeves to top sleeves, along both seams.

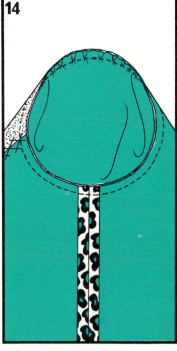

14 R.S. together, match notches and tack sleeves into position, adjusting ease. Stitch.

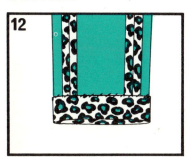

12 Turn up 1½ in. hem on sleeve bottoms. Slip stitch into position.

13 Using running stitch, sew a gathering thread, along upper sleeve head.

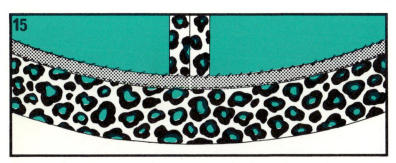

15 Turn up hem of coat to fit child. Use seam binding on hem if you prefer. (See 'hems' page 10.) Pin in position, tack and slip stitch into position.

16 Cut out lining and make up—R.S. together, stitch shoulder seams and then continue as for coat on side seams and sleeves.

Turn up hem of lining so that it is 1 in. above the hem of the coat. Tack and slip stitch this hem.

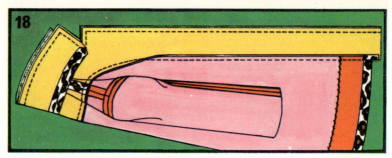

R.S. coat facing and lining together, stitch lining to facing starting at the hem and continuing round the neck to the other hem.

Turn to right side out. Slip stitch undersleeve of coat to undersleeve of lining at armhole seam, so lining does not slip round.

Slip stitch shoulder seams of coat to coat lining, to hold in position and prevent lining from slipping.

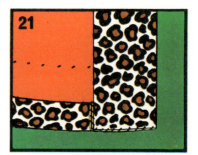

Turn back front facings of coat and slip stitch into position at hem.

Turn sleeve lining hem to W.S. and slip stitch to coat sleeve. Allow some ease so sleeve hangs correctly.

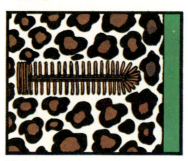

Make hand buttonholes using buttonhole twist. (On right front for a girl and left front for a boy.)

Sew buttons in place. Work a loop at top of facing same side as buttonholes. Sew on button on opposite side.

HAT: R.S. together, pin, tack and stitch sections together to make crown. Make lining in same way.

W.S. together, place lining inside cap. Tack around raw edges to hold lining and cap together.

3 Run a gathering thread along 2 panels. (This will be the peak).

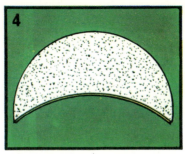

4 Place interfacing on W.S. of one peak shape.

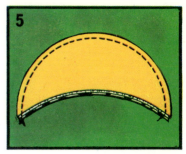

5 Place R.S. of peak together and stitch through the two pieces of peak and one layer of interfacing.

6 Turn peak to R.S. Pin to R.S. of crown along gathering thread. A seam of crown should be in centre of peak. Tack.

7 Pin elastic to remainder of crown edge. Stretch elastic as you pin. Stitch both sides of elastic.

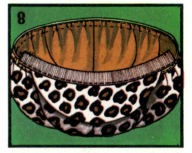

8 Stitch petersham to peak, finishing ¾ in. either side of peak and overlapping elastic. Hand sew corners of petersham to inside.

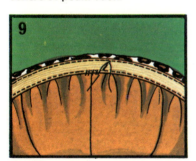

9 By hand, sew the centre back of the elastic to the inside of the crown.

The hat pattern is for a head approximate size 21 in. For a smaller size, when making the pattern, reduce the width of each of the eight sections by the desired amount, and use a correspondingly smaller amount of elastic. For a larger size increase both width of crown sections and length of elastic.

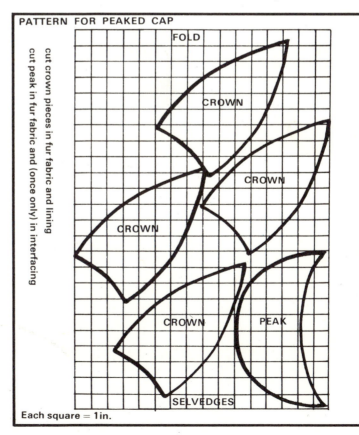

PATTERN FOR PEAKED CAP

cut crown pieces in fur fabric and lining
cut peak in fur fabric and (once only) in interfacing

FOLD

CROWN

CROWN

CROWN

CROWN   PEAK

SELVEDGES

Each square = 1 in.

Zip-fronted Shirt

This little shirt will suit boys and girls alike. Remember to take extra care when putting in the zip as it is the main feature of the garment.

TO ADJUST YOUR PATTERN:
The pattern is in Size 6.
For a size larger make the following adjustments:
FRONT: Widen pattern at side seam by $\frac{1}{4}$ in.
           Widen pattern at armhole level by $\frac{1}{4}$ in.
           Adjust neck to fit your child.
           Lengthen shirt by 1 in.
BACK: As for front.
SLEEVE: Widen sleeves by $\frac{1}{4}$ in. at either side at underarm seam.
           Lengthen sleeves by 1 in.
For a size smaller make the same adjustments but as reductions.

YOU WILL NEED:
$1\frac{1}{2}$ yds 36 in. wide
   lightweight jersey
Matching sewing thread
Matching zip

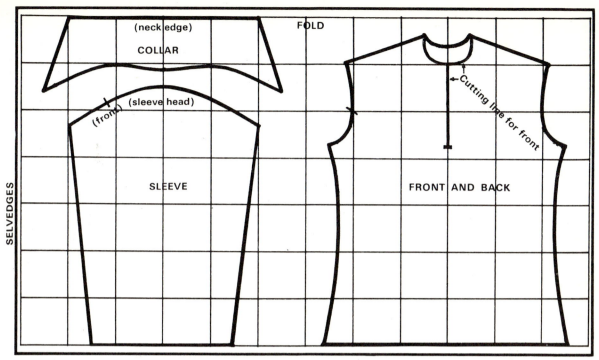

PATTERN FOR ZIP-FRONT SHIRT   Each square = 3 inches

Labels within pattern: (neck edge), COLLAR, FOLD, (sleeve head), (front), SLEEVE, FRONT AND BACK, Cutting line for front, SELVEDGES

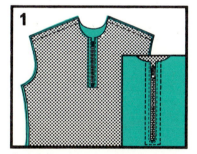

1 Carefully insert zip at centre front. R.S. together, pin, tack and stitch shoulder seams. Top-stitch seams on R.S. garment.

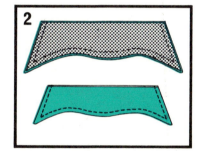

2 R.S. together, stitch collar to undercollar. Turn to right side. Press and top stitch.

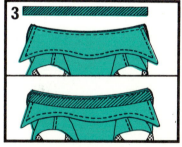

3 R.S. together, tack collar to shirt. Cut crossway strip 1 in. wide, same length as collar. Stitch edge to collar edge.

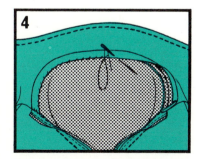

4 Turn opposite edge over and slipstitch to cover raw edges of collar and top of shirt. With R.S. together, stitch in sleeves.

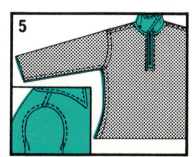

5 Top stitch round armhole seams on R.S. garment. Then W.S. together, stitch side seams and underarm seams.

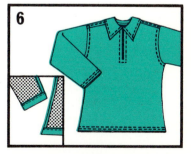

6 Turn up 1 in. hem on sleeves and bottom of shirt. Top stitch two rows of stitching round each hem on R.S. garment.

47

Fur-Fronted Jacket and Cap

What little boy wouldn't be thrilled with this jacket and hat?
Quick and easy to make, the fronts are imitation fur.

TO ADJUST YOUR PATTERN:
The jacket is in Size 6.
For a larger size make the following adjustments:
BACK: Increase neck length by $\frac{1}{16}$ in.
            Increase shoulder seam by $\frac{1}{8}$ in.
            Increase total length by $\frac{3}{4}$ in.
            Deepen armhole by $\frac{1}{2}$ in.
FRONT: As for back.
SLEEVE: Widen sleeve by $\frac{1}{4}$ in. either side.
            Lengthen sleeves by $\frac{3}{4}$ in.
For a smaller size decrease by a corresponding amount.
The hat fits a 21 in. head.

YOU WILL NEED:
for jacket:
1 yd 36 in. wide fabric
  (gaberdine or similar)
$\frac{1}{2}$ yd 36 in. wide fur fabric
Matching Sewing Thread
Purchased Knitted Ribbing
Velcro

for hat:
$\frac{2}{3}$ yd 36 in. wide fabric
  (as jacket)
Purchased Knitted Fabric
Matching Sewing Thread
Buckles

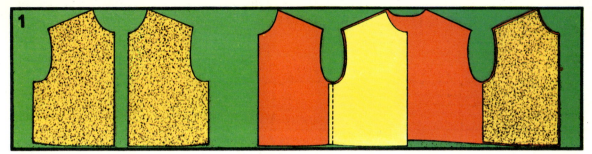

FUR FRONTED JACKET: Place W.S. of fur fronts on R.S. jacket fronts. Fold fur to the back of the jacket, to find where side seam will be, as shown. Stitch along side seams (with R.S. fur to R.S. *back* of jacket) and fold fur back to jacket fronts.

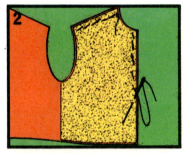

Tack shoulder and front edges of fur to jacket to hold in place.

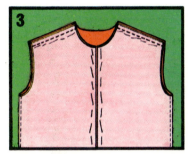

R.S. together, pin, tack and stitch shoulder seams, including fur fronts.

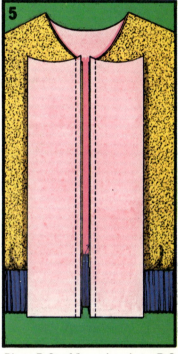

Place R.S. of front bands to R.S. of jacket fronts (on top of fur). Stitch in place.

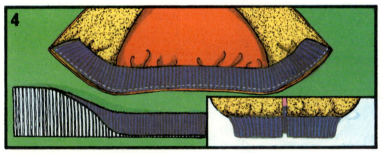

Cut a strip of knitted rib 16 in × 5 in. Fold in half and stitch raw edges to R.S. lower edge of jacket.

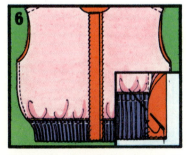

Fold half of each band over to W.S. Turn under raw edges and slip stitch in place.

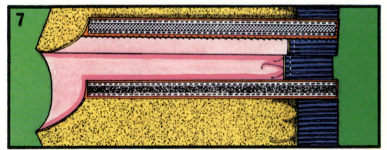

Sew Velcro to R.S. of right hand front band and W.S. of left hand front band, following maker's instructions.

PATTERN FOR BOYS FUR-FRONTED JACKET

Each square = 3 inches

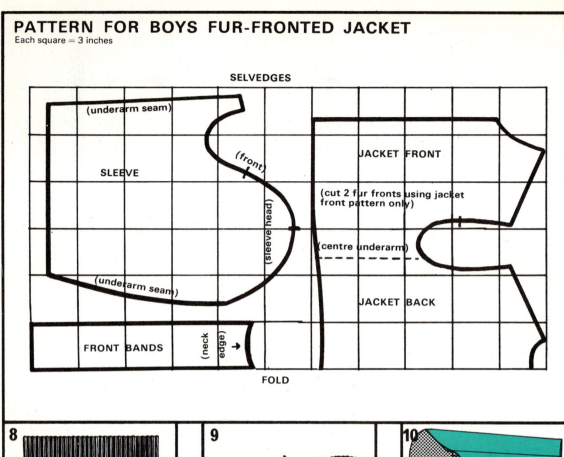

SELVEDGES

(underarm seam)

SLEEVE

(front)

(sleeve head)

(underarm seam)

JACKET FRONT

(cut 2 fur fronts using jacket front pattern only)

(centre underarm)

JACKET BACK

FRONT BANDS

(neck edge) →

FOLD

8

Cut a strip of knitted rib $12\frac{1}{2}$ in. × 3 in. Place one raw edge to R.S. of neck edge. Pin, tack and stitch in place.

9

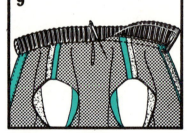

Turn over to W.S. so approximately 1 in. shows on R.S. Turn under to cover raw edges, and slip stitch in place.

10

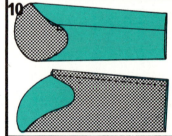

R.S. inside, pin, tack and stitch along sleeve seams.

11

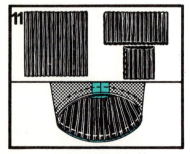

Cut 2 strips of knitted rib 5 in. × 5 in. Fold in half and stitch down long edge. Fold over. Stitch sleeves at cuff to R.S.

12

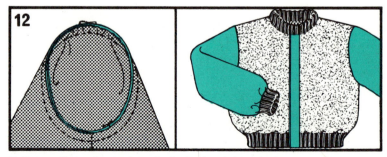

R.S. together, pin, tack and stitch sleeve into jacket.

1

CAP: R.S. together, tack and stitch side crown to top crown, matching dots. Make up crown lining in same way.

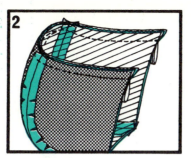

2

Place R.S. crown and lining together. Fold knitted fabric lengthways, insert between, all raw edges together. Stitch.

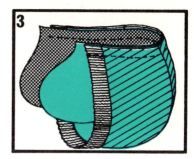

3

Turn hat right side out, so knitted fabric is on edge. R.S. together, tack and stitch crown to neckband.

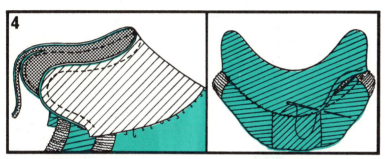

4

R.S. together, place neckband lining on neckband. Tack and stitch round edges (except at base of crown). Trim turning and turn lining to W.S. Turn in neck edge and slip stitch lining to base of crown.

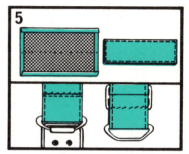

5

Fold straps lengthwise, W.S. inside and stitch along both edges. Fold in raw edges at end and stitch. Sew on buckles.

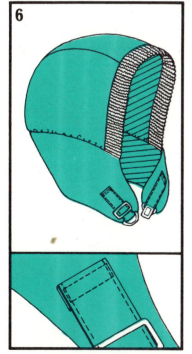

6

Sew straps and buckles to hat.

PATTERN FOR HAT

Each square = 3 inches

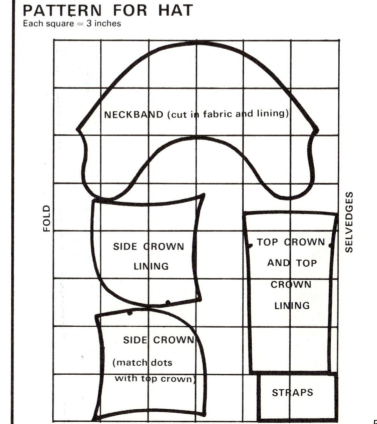

NECKBAND (cut in fabric and lining)

FOLD

SIDE CROWN LINING

TOP CROWN AND TOP CROWN LINING

SELVEDGES

SIDE CROWN (match dots with top crown)

STRAPS

Cape for Rainy Days

Colourful PVC helps to brighten up those cloudy skies, and boys and girls alike will keep dry beneath this lovely cape and hood.

TO ADJUST YOUR PATTERN:
The pattern is in Size 5.
For a size larger make the following adjustments:
BACK CAPE: Increase neck length by $\frac{1}{16}$ in.
                          Increase cape length by 2 in.
FRONT CAPE: As for back.
HOOD: Increase hood centre width by $\frac{1}{8}$ in. either side.
For cape size 4 decrease by corresponding amount.

YOU WILL NEED:
$2\frac{1}{2}$ yds 36 in. wide fabric
     (PVC or similar)
$\frac{1}{2}$ yd 36 in. wide lining fabric
Matching Sewing Thread
Velcro
Glue (Copydex is best)

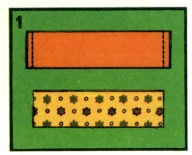

1 R.S. together, fold pocket flap in half and stitch along short sides. Turn to right side out.

2 R.S. together, stitch pocket flaps to back of cape.

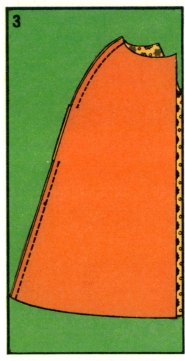

3 R.S. together, stitch cape fronts to cape backs, leaving pocket flap free.

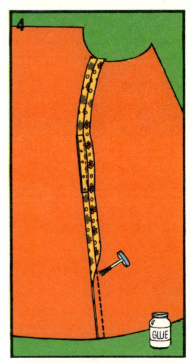

4 Glue seams down on wrong side to keep them flat. (Follow maker's instructions on adhesive carefully.)

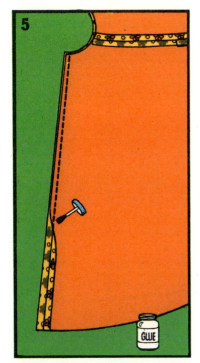

5 R.S. together, stitch centre back seam. Glue seam turnings down.

6 Turn up hem to fit child round bottom of raincoat and glue in place.

7 Fold fronts of cape to inside along fold lines marked. (Note this is not the centre front line.)

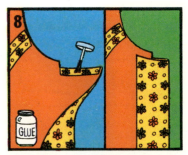

8 Fold $\frac{1}{2}$ in. at top of facing to inside. Clip edge so it lies flat and glue in position.

PATTERN FOR RAINCAPE

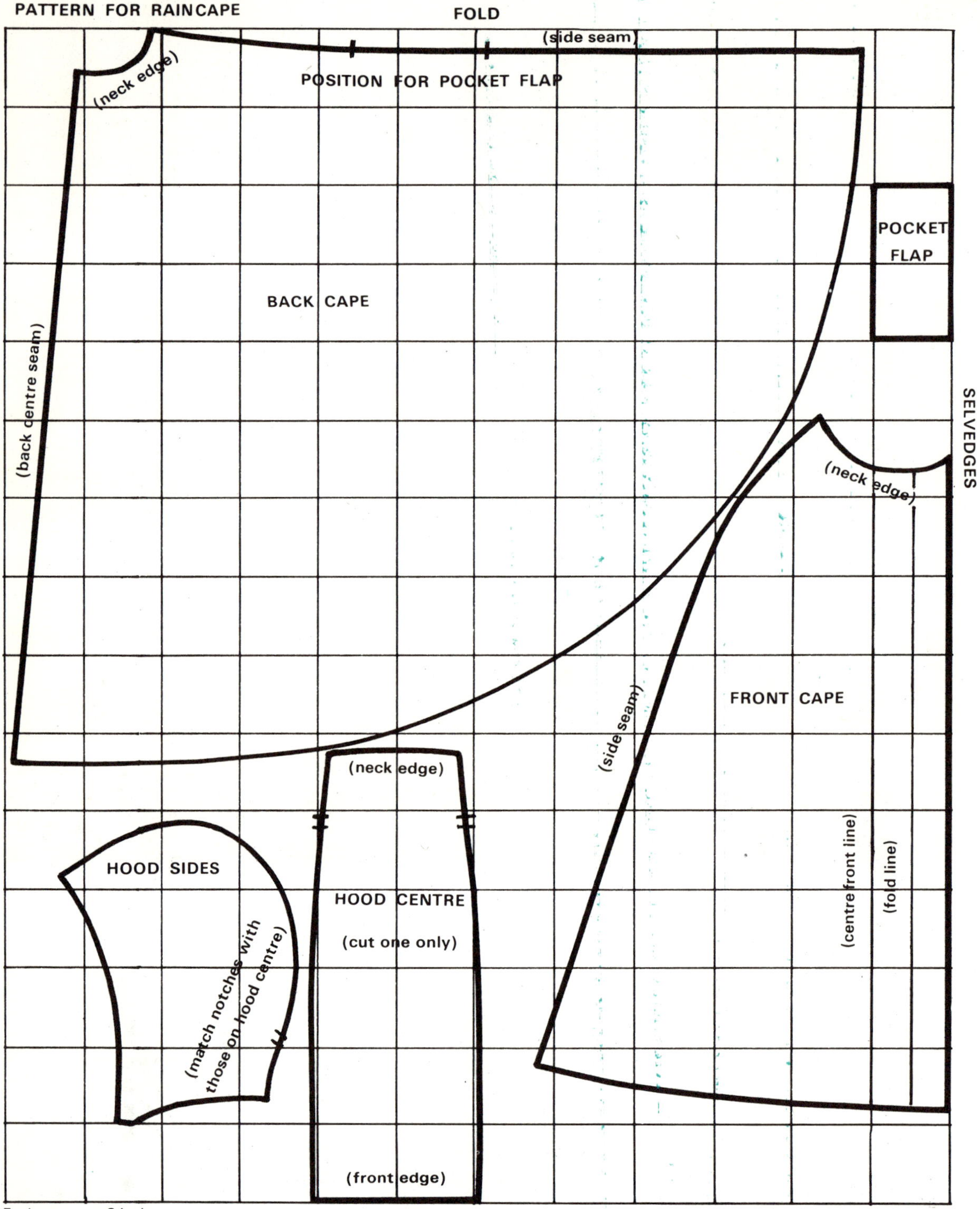

FOLD

(side seam)

(neck edge)

POSITION FOR POCKET FLAP

POCKET FLAP

BACK CAPE

(back centre seam)

SELVEDGES

(neck edge)

FRONT CAPE

(side seam)

(neck edge)

(centre front line)

(fold line)

HOOD SIDES

HOOD CENTRE

(cut one only)

(match notches with those on hood centre)

(front edge)

Each square = 3 inches

9

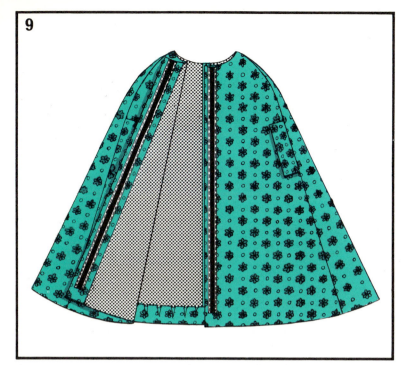

Stitch Velcro ½ in. from edge on R.S. of left front of cape. Stitch ½ in. in from edge on W.S. of right front.

10

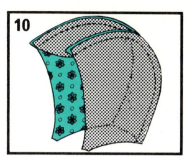

R.S. together, stitch hood sides to hood centre, easing round curves.

11

Glue seams to keep them flat as you did on cape seams.

12

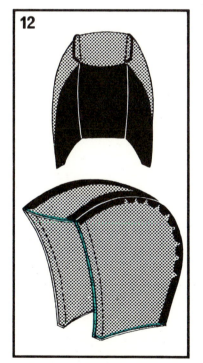

Make up hood lining in the same way, but do not glue seams. R.S. together, stitch lining to hood round front seam.

13

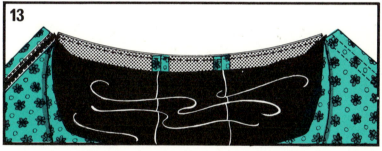

Turn lining to inside. With R.S. of hood to R.S. of cape, stitch together round neck.

14

Turn under raw edges of lining and slip stitch onto neck seam.

Night-time for Little Girls

Refreshingly cool and pretty, any little girl will love this dreamy nightie. Our instructions tell you how to make a pair of baby doll pyjamas too using the same pattern.

TO ADJUST YOUR PATTERN:
The pattern is in Size 6.
To make the pattern a size larger adjust as follows:
FRONT: Lengthen nightdress by 3 in.
             Widen by $\frac{1}{2}$ in.
BACK: As front.

SLEEVES: Lengthen sleeves by 1 in.
              Widen sleeves by $\frac{1}{2}$ in.
To make a size smaller make the same adjustments but as reductions. However, for one smaller size use the sleeve pattern of a size 6.

YOU WILL NEED:
$2\frac{1}{8}$ yds 36 in. wide fabric
   (Make sure it is
   'Flame-free').
Matching Sewing Thread
Shirring elastic
Lace

NIGHTDRESS: R.S. of frill together, stitch the seams. Turn under a small hem and tack the lace in position as close to the edge as possible. Stitch in place.

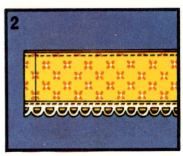

Run a gathering thread round the other edge of the frill.

R.S. together, pin, tack and stitch side seams of nightdress.

Pull up gathers of frill and adjust so it fits evenly round bottom of nightdress. R.S. together, pin, tack and stitch in place.

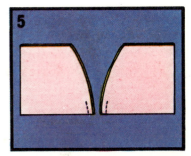

R.S. inside, stitch underarm seam of sleeves.

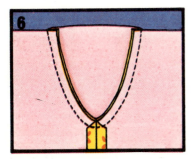

R.S. together, stitch sleeves to nightdress.

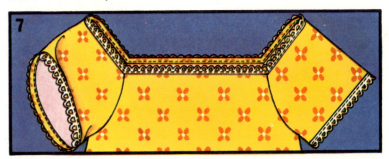

Turn under a small hem on bottom of sleeves and right round neck. Pin and tack lace close to the edge and stitch in position.

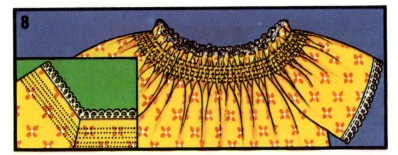

Put shirring elastic on the bobbin of your machine (follow maker's instructions). Sew five rows of shirring round the neck of the nightdress $\frac{1}{4}$ in. apart. The first line should be $\frac{3}{4}$ in. from the edge.

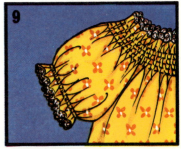

Stitch 2 rows or shirring elastic round sleeve hem $\frac{1}{2}$ in. from the edge.

PATTERN FOR NIGHTDRESS AND BABYDOLL PYJAMAS

Each square = 3 inches

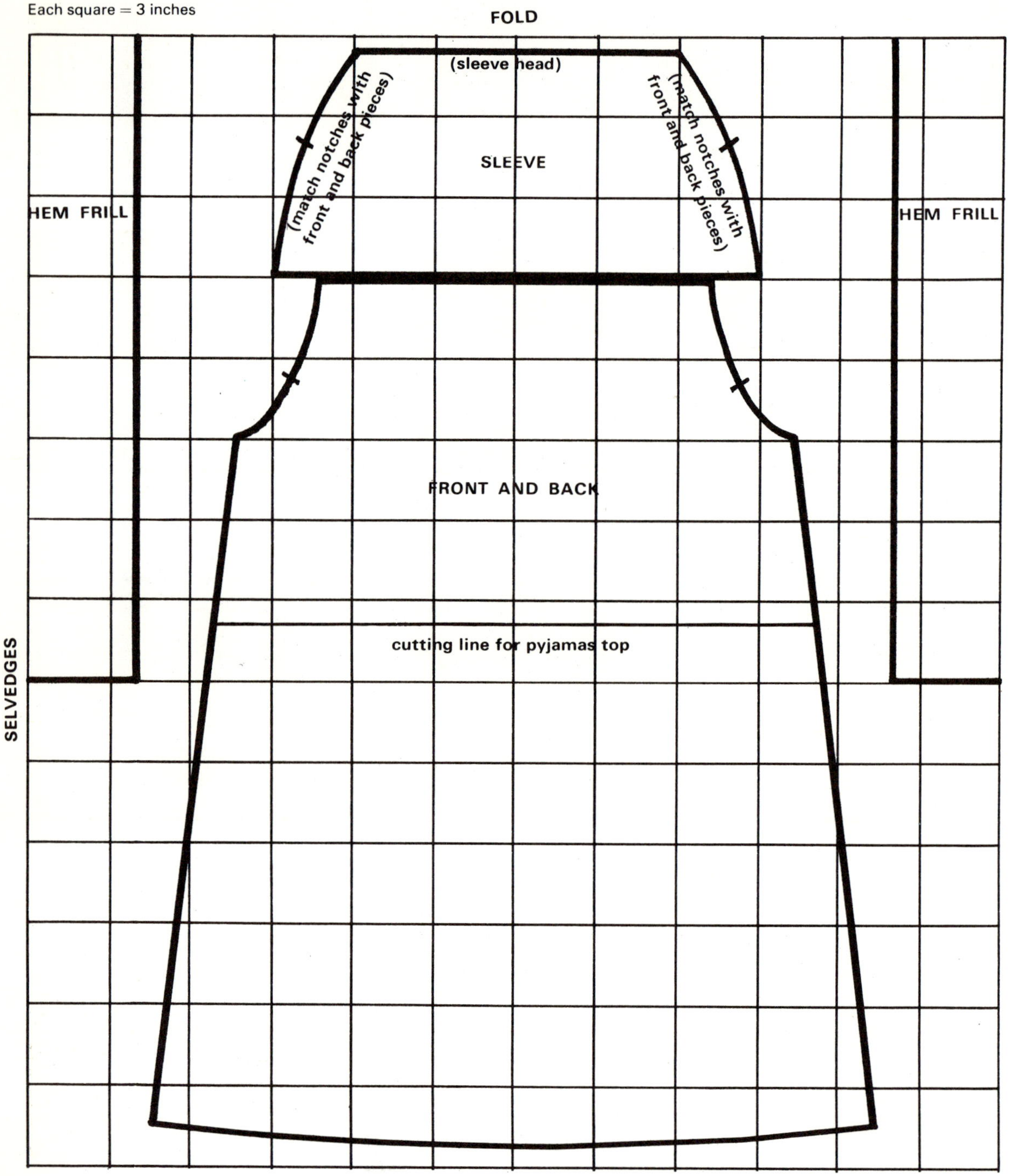

FOLD

(sleeve head)

SLEEVE

(match notches with front and back pieces)

(match notches with front and back pieces)

HEM FRILL

HEM FRILL

SELVEDGES

FRONT AND BACK

cutting line for pyjamas top

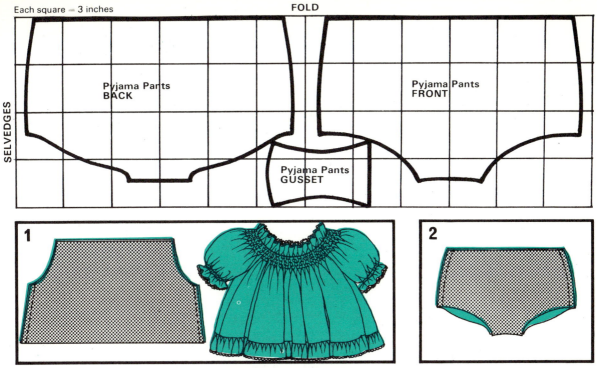

SELVEDGES

Pyjama Pants
BACK

Pyjama Pants
FRONT

Pyjama Pants
GUSSET

1

PYJAMAS: Follow the pattern for the nightdress, but cut out tops on the dotted line. Then make up in exactly the same way as the nightdress.

2

Pants: R.S. together, pin, tack and stitch side seams.

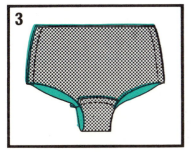

3

R.S. together, pin, tack and stitch gusset to pants.

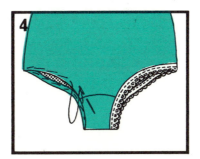

4

Turn small hem to W.S. round legs. Pin, tack and stitch lace in position.

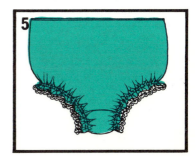

5

Stitch 2 rows of shirring elastic round legs, $\frac{1}{2}$ in. from edge.

6

Fold $1\frac{1}{4}$ in. at top of pants to wrong side and hem down leaving a small opening.

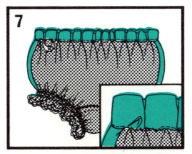

7

Cut elastic to fit child's waist. Thread round top of pants and stitch ends together. Slip stitch opening.

Judo Pyjamas and Bathrobe

These judo pyjamas will be such a favourite, they will doubtless make bedtime much easier! The pattern for the top can be used to make a lovely bathrobe.

TO ADJUST YOUR PATTERN:
The pattern is in Size 6.
For a size larger make the following adjustments:
Jacket
FRONT: Widen side seams by $\frac{1}{4}$ in.
Widen at shoulder seams by $\frac{1}{4}$ in.
Lengthen by $1\frac{1}{4}$ in.
BACK: As for front.
SLEEVE: Widen each side by $\frac{1}{4}$ in.
Lengthen by $1\frac{1}{4}$ in.
Trousers
Widen trousers at crutch level by $\frac{1}{4}$ in. each side.
Extend waist upwards by 1 in.
Lengthen by $1\frac{1}{2}$ in.
For a smaller size make the same adjustments but as reductions.

YOU WILL NEED:
for pyjamas
3 yds 36 in. wide fabric
$\frac{1}{2}$ yd 36 in. wide fabric for belt
Matching Sewing Thread
2 Buttons
Waist Elastic

for bathrobe
2 yds 36 in. wide fabric (preferably towelling)
Matching Sewing Thread

JUDO PYJAMAS AND BATHROBE: R.S. together, pin, tack and stitch shoulder seams on the jacket and facing.

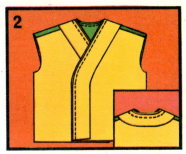

Stitch R.S. of facing to W.S. of fronts and neck of jacket.

Turn facing to the front of garment. Turn under raw edges, pin, tack and top stitch 2 rows as shown.

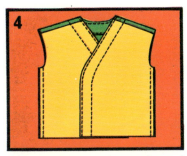

R.S. together, pin, tack and stitch side seams.

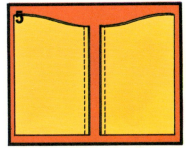

R.S. together, pin, tack and stitch underarm sleeve seams.

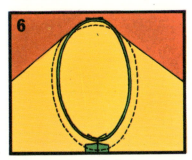

R.S. together, stitch sleeves into jacket.

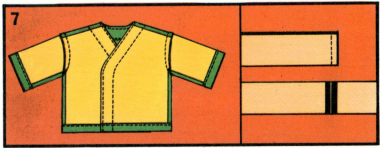

Turn under a 1½ in. hem round bottom of jacket and sleeves. Stitch in place. Cut belt material into 7 in. wide strips and join to make a belt 54 in. long.

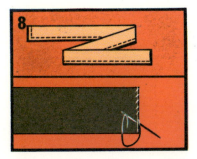

Fold in half lengthways, stitch round leaving a small opening. Pull belt through to R.S. and slip stitch opening.

To make trousers: R.S. together, pin, tack and stitch back seam of trousers.

Turn a ½ in. hem to wrong side of trouser top and tack in place.

PATTERN FOR JUDO PYJAMAS

Each square = 3 inches

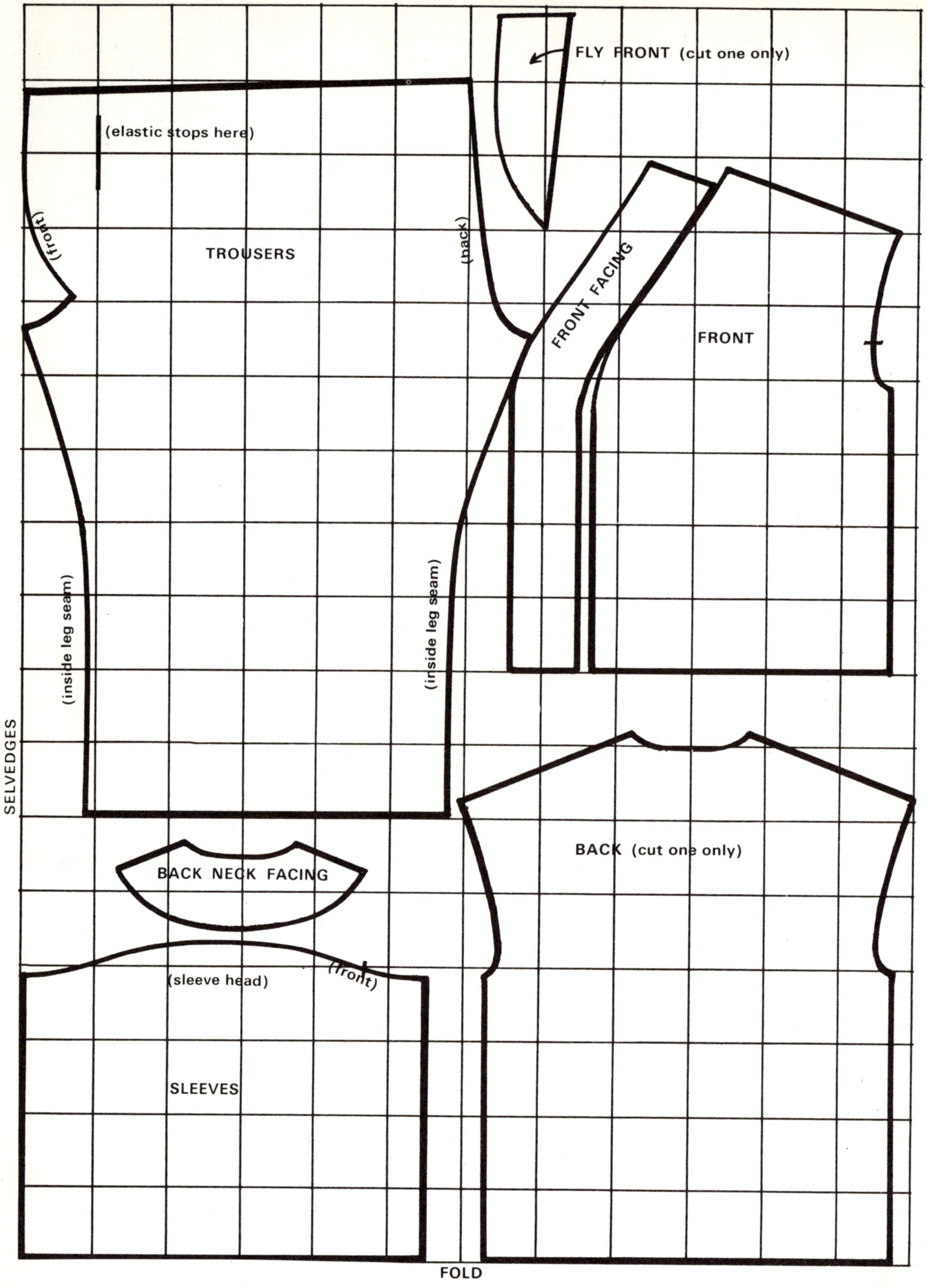

FLY FRONT (cut one only)

(elastic stops here)

(front)

TROUSERS

(back)

FRONT FACING

FRONT

(inside leg seam)

(inside leg seam)

SELVEDGES

BACK NECK FACING

BACK (cut one only)

(sleeve head)

(front)

SLEEVES

FOLD

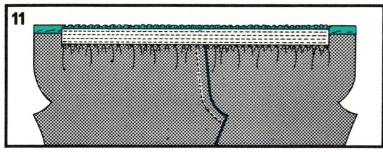

11 Measure child's waist, and cut elastic to fit comfortably. Lay elastic along top of trousers and stitch it $\frac{3}{8}$ in. from the top edge stretching it as you go. Stitch 3 more parallel rows, approximately $\frac{3}{8}$ in. apart.

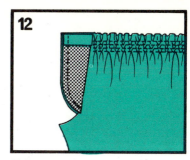

12 R.S. together, pin, tack and stitch fly front to left hand side of pyjama front.

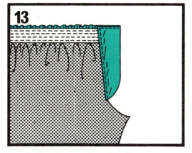

13 Turn facing to back of garment. Turn under to cover raw edges and tack. Machine a line of stitching along turning.

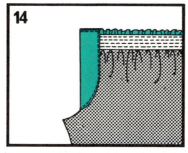

14 Turn under fly piece on right hand side of pyjamas. Turn to cover raw edge, tack and machine 1 row along turning.

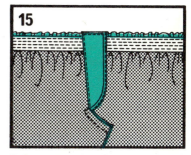

15 R.S. together, pin, tack and stitch along crutch seam, overlapping left to right facing.

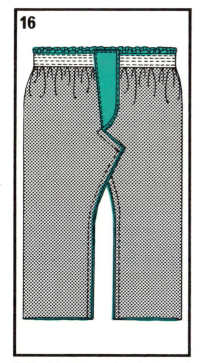

16 R.S. together, pin, tack and stitch along inside leg seam.

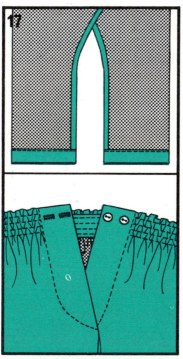

17 Turn under $1\frac{1}{2}$ in. hem on legs and stitch. Make two buttonholes on top right hand side and sew buttons on left front facing.

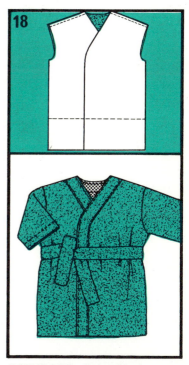

18 BATHROBE: Extend jacket pattern to desired length and make in exactly the same way using a towelling material.

Sunny Day Clothes

Skirts and a sun dress for cool wear on sunny days. Best of all—they are quick and simple to make. The sun dress is made from strips of material—no need even for a pattern! (Instructions for sundress are on the opposite page.)

TO ADJUST YOUR PATTERN:
The Sun dress is Size 5.
For a larger size increase the size of the square by $\frac{1}{2}$ in. all round. Increase the skirts to required length. For smaller sizes decrease accordingly.

Skirts:
The pattern is Size 8.
For smaller or larger sizes, adjust pieces to child's waist size and height.

YOU WILL NEED:
for the sundress:
1 yd 36 in. wide fabric
$\frac{1}{2}$ yd 36 in. wide fabric—
 contrasting print
$\frac{3}{4}$ yd 36 in. wide fabric—
 contrasting print
Matching Sewing Thread
$\frac{1}{2}$ in. wide elastic for waist

for the long skirt:
$2\frac{1}{2}$ yd 36 in. wide fabric
Matching Sewing Thread
6 in. zip. Press studs

for the short skirt:
1 yd 36 in. wide fabric
Matching Sewing Thread
2 in. wide ribbed elastic

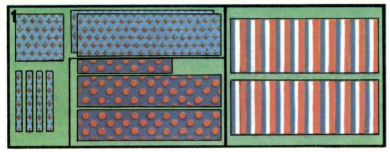

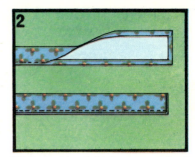

SUN DRESS: From 1st print, cut a 12 in. square, 4 strips 1½ in.×15 in. and 2 strips 10½ in.×15 in. for bodice, ties and middle skirt. From 2nd print cut 2 strips 7 in.×36 in. and 1 strip 3 in.×28 in. for top skirt and waist band. From 3rd print cut 2 pieces 13½ in.×36 in. for lower skirt.

W.S. inside, fold in one end of each tie. Fold in raw edges right along. Pin, tack and slip stitch sides together.

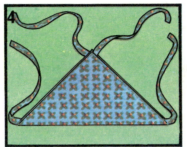

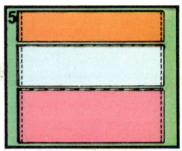

Turn ¾ in. turnings to W.S. all round the 12 in. square. Then fold square crosswise as shown.

Insert raw edges of ties at top point and sides. Pin, tack and stitch firmly in place. Stitch along open sides close to edge.

R.S. together, stitch along side seams of each of the 3 skirt lengths.

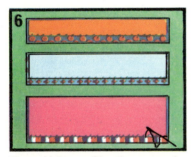

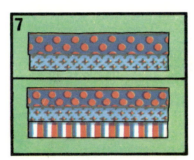

Turn under a 2 in. hem to the wrong side on each piece. Pin, tack and slip stitch in place.

W.S. inside, place top skirt over middle skirt and both skirts over lower one. Pin at top to hold together.

Tun a gathering thread at top of all skirts and draw up to fit waistband.

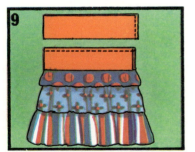

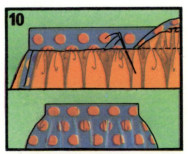

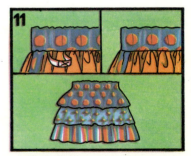

Stitch side seam of waistband and then, with R.S. together, pin, tack and stitch waistband to top of all skirts.

Fold waistband over to wrong side of skirt. Turn over to cover raw edges and slip stitch, leaving a small opening.

Insert elastic to fit comfortably round child's waist. Stitch ends together. Slip stitch opening in waistband.

PATTERN FOR LONG SKIRT WITH FRILL

Each square = 3 inches

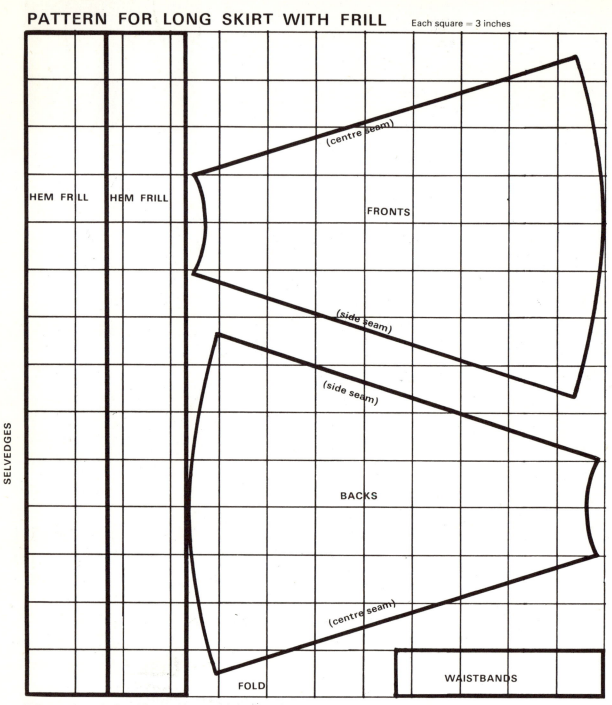

HEM FRILL   HEM FRILL

(centre seam)

FRONTS

(side seam)

(side seam)

BACKS

(centre seam)

FOLD

WAISTBANDS

SELVEDGES

N.B. pattern only fits this way if material does not have a
one-way pattern.

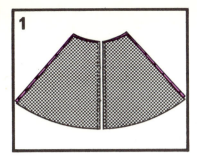

LONG SKIRT: R.S. together, pin, tack and stitch front skirts and back skirts down centre seams.

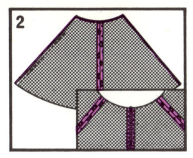

Pin, tack and stitch left hand side seam in the same way and insert zip.

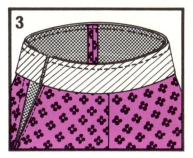

Pin, tack and stitch other side seam. R.S. together, pin, tack and stitch 1 edge of waistband round top of skirt.

Fold waistband over to wrong side, turn to cover raw edge and slip stitch in place. Slip stitch ends. Sew on press studs.

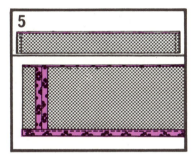

R.S. together, stitch side seams of hem frill together. Turn a small hem to W.S. on one edge and slip stitch in place.

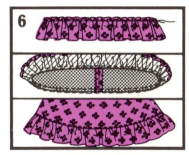

Gather other side. R.S. together, adjusting gathers, pin, tack and stitch frill to lower edge of skirt.

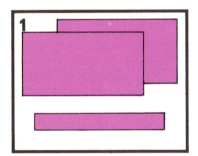

SHORT SKIRT: From a square yard of material, cut 2 strips 18 in. × 32 in. The remaining strip (4 in. × 36 in.) is for the waistband.

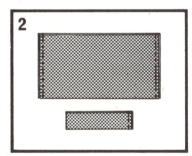

R.S. of large strips together, stitch down shorter seams. Pin, tack and stitch waistband seam in the same way.

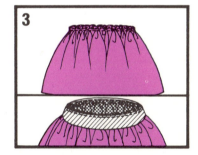

Run a gathering thread round top of skirt. R.S. together, pin, tack and stitch to the waistband.

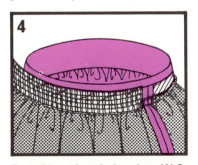

Turn 1 in. of waistband to W.S. at top. Pin elastic $\frac{1}{2}$ in. from top edge (inside skirt).

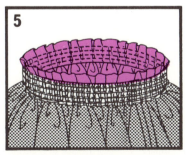

Machine stitch elastic to waistband, stretching elastic as you stitch. Stitch 4 rows $\frac{1}{4}$ in. distances apart.

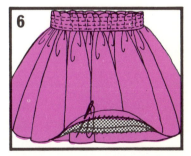

Turn a $2\frac{1}{2}$ in. hem to W.S. at bottom of skirt. Slip stitch in place.

Party Dress for Sophisticates

A dream dress—romantic and pretty, but just right for an 8–10 year old. Make it from light cotton for a floating effect.

TO ADJUST YOUR PATTERN:
The pattern is in Size 8.
For a larger size make the following adjustments:

FRONT BODICE: Widen chest by $\frac{1}{2}$ in.
Widen at centre armhole level by $\frac{1}{4}$ in.
Lengthen shoulder by $\frac{1}{8}$ in.
Lengthen bodice by $\frac{1}{2}$ in.
Deepen armhole by $\frac{1}{4}$ in.
BACK BODICE: As for front.
FRONT SKIRT: Lengthen by $1\frac{1}{2}$ in.
Width remains the same.
BACK SKIRT: As front skirt.
SLEEVE: All sections of sleeve widen by $\frac{1}{2}$ in.
All sections of sleeve lengthen by $\frac{3}{8}$ in.
BOW, BELT & COLLAR: Remain the same.
For one size smaller make the adjustments as reductions.

YOU WILL NEED:
$4\frac{2}{3}$ yds 36 in. wide fabric
1 yd 36 in. wide contrasting plain fabric
Matching Sewing Thread
14 in. zip
$\frac{1}{4}$ in. wide elastic
Bias Binding

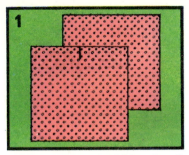

LONG PARTY DRESS: Cut 2 lengths of fabric 36 in. square for skirt pieces. Cut a small slit at centre of one for zip.

R.S. together, pin, tack and stitch skirt side seams.

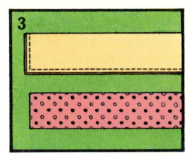

R.S. together, stitch long edges and one short edge of belt pieces. Turn to right side out and press.

Stitch darts shown on pattern in front and back bodices.

R.S. together, pin, tack and stitch shoulder and bodice side seams, with belt ties in place at waist edge.

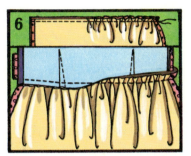

Run a gathering thread round top of skirt. R.S. together, pin, tack and stitch skirt to bodice, adjusting gathers evenly.

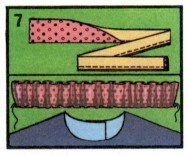

W.S. inside, fold collar and turn in ends. Run gathering thread along raw edges. Draw up to fit neck.

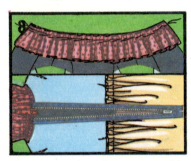

Pin and tack collar to outside neck. Insert zip in centre back, extending slit in skirt if necessary.

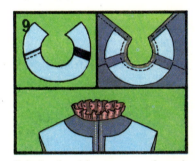

Stitch shoulder seams of neck facing. R.S. together, pin, tack and stitch facing to collar and dress. Turn facing to W.S.

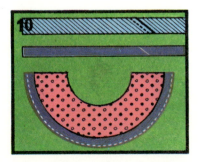

Join contrast colour crossway strips to trim lower sleeves. Fold lengthways, press, stitch to R.S. top of lower sleeve.

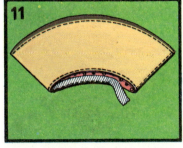

R.S. together, stitch seam of lower sleeves (crossway strip folded to R.S.). Sew bias binding round cuff edge. Turn to inside.

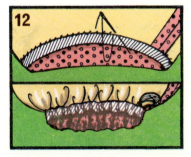

Slip stitch in place leaving opening for elastic. Thread elastic through and sew ends securely. Slip stitch opening.

PATTERN FOR LONG DRESS *PRINTED FABRIC*

Each square = 3 inches

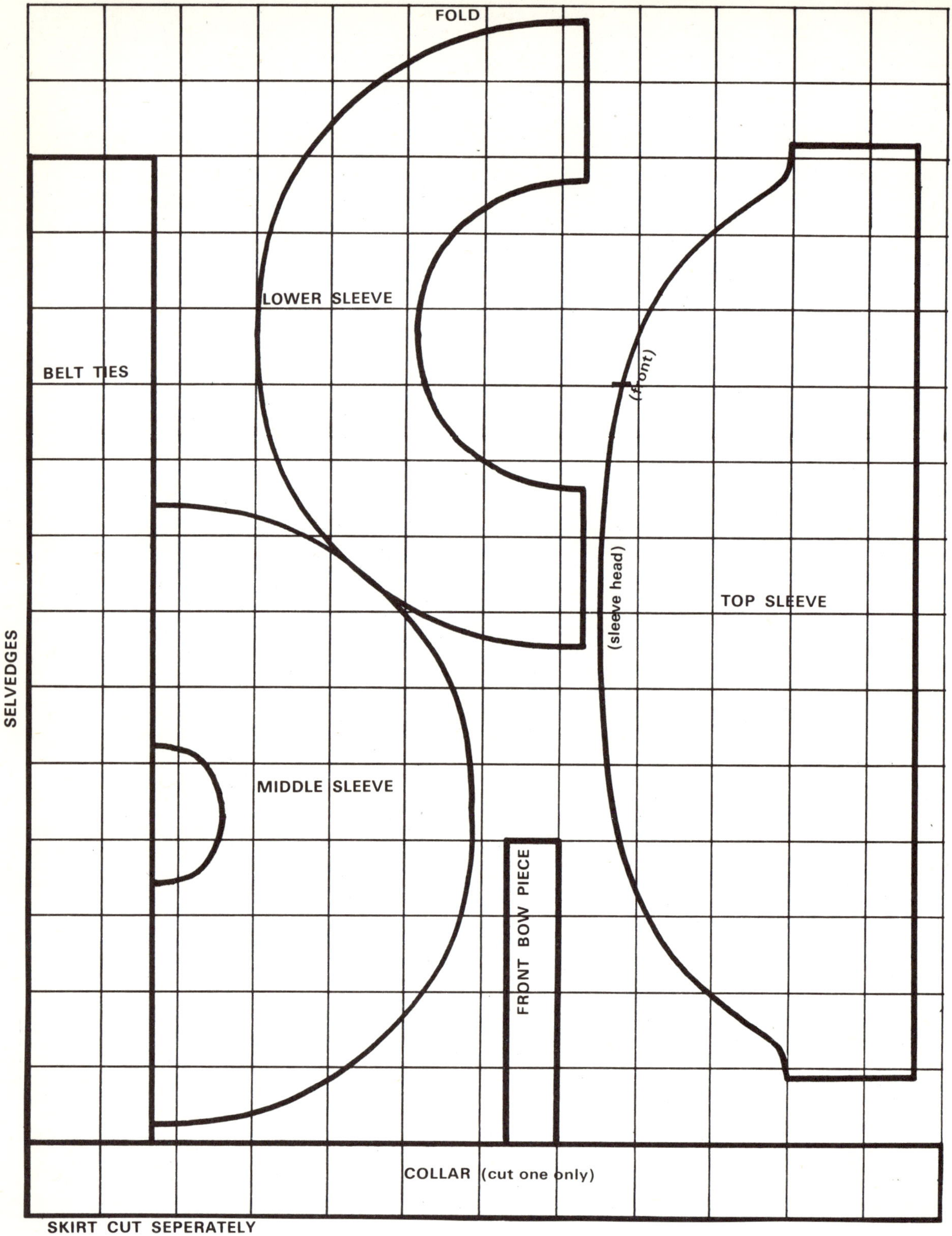

FOLD
LOWER SLEEVE
BELT TIES
(front)
(sleeve head)
TOP SLEEVE
SELVEDGES
MIDDLE SLEEVE
FRONT BOW PIECE
COLLAR (cut one only)

SKIRT CUT SEPERATELY

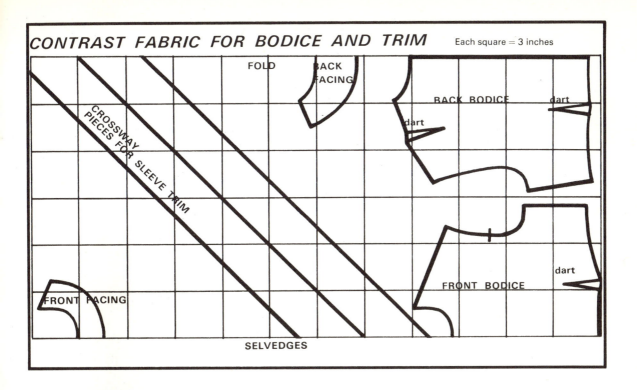

CONTRAST FABRIC FOR BODICE AND TRIM — Each square = 3 inches

FOLD
BACK FACING
BACK BODICE — dart
dart
CROSSWAY PIECES FOR SLEEVE TRIM
FRONT BODICE — dart
FRONT FACING
SELVEDGES

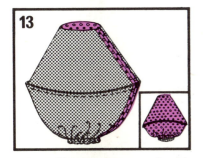

13 R.S. inside, stitch seam of middle sleeves. R.S. together, stitch middle to lower sleeves (strip stands out on R.S.).

14 Work smocking on upper sleeve as shown on page 13. R.S. inside, stitch top sleeve seam, then top sleeve to middle sleeve.

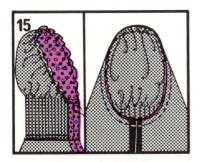

15 Run gathering thread round head of top sleeve. Draw up to fit armhole. Pin, tack and stitch to dress adjusting gathers.

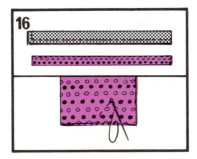

16 Fold bow piece R.S. inside, stitch along long edge and one short edge. Turn to right side and slip stitch end.

17 Tie into a bow and sew at centre of bodice, just below collar. Turn up hem on skirt to fit. Slip stitch in place.

Smart Check Trousers

A terrific pair of trousers that are ideal for girls and boys. The elasticated waist means no fussing to put in zips. Easy to make and great to wear.

TO ADJUST YOUR PATTERN:
The pattern is in Size 6.
For a size larger make the following adjustments.
Lengthen trouser by $1\frac{1}{2}$ in. crutch to hem.
Extend crutch to waist seam upwards by $\frac{1}{2}$ in.
Cut the pattern along the "side seam" level and open out by $\frac{3}{4}$ in.
Redraw outline of pattern.
For a size smaller make the same adjustments but as reductions.

YOU WILL NEED:
1 yd 54 in. wide fabric
Matching sewing thread
Elastic braid trim

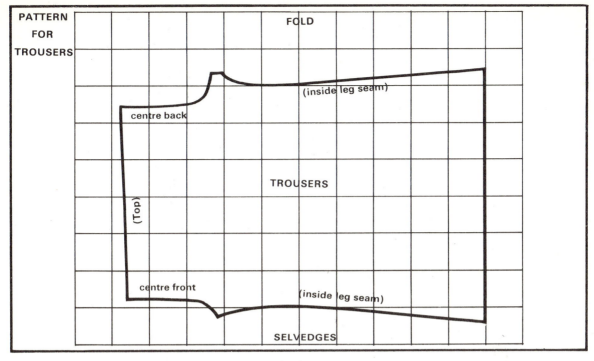

PATTERN
FOR
TROUSERS

FOLD

(inside leg seam)

centre back

(Top)

TROUSERS

centre front

(inside leg seam)

SELVEDGES

(NB trousers are cut in 2 pieces—there are no side seams)   Each square = 3 inches

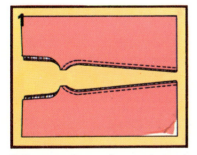

1 R.S. together, pin, tack and stitch leg seams.

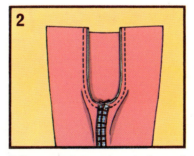

2 R.S. together, pin, tack and stitch crutch seams.

3 Cut elastic braid trim to required length for waist fitting. Overlap ends and stitch together.

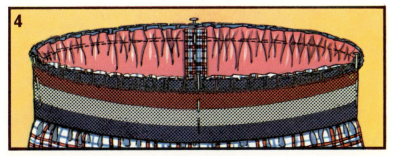

4 Divide waistband into four. R.S. together, pin each point at centre front and back and left and right sides. Tack and stitch at top and bottom of elastic stretching it as you sew.

5 Turn up hems round bottom of legs to fit child and slip stitch in place.

Knitting and Crochet

Garments in this section of the book have all been made by hand knitting, and some of them are finished off with crochet stitches. On this and the next few pages we give implicit instructions for how to knit and crochet as well as some general points of pressing and sewing up of garments and checking knitting tension. If you already know how to knit and crochet, we would still advise you to read the general notes which ensure the very best results for knitted garments. In all our patterns figures in brackets refer to the larger sizes respectively. Where only one figure is given, it refers to all sizes.

CASTING ON

Begin by leaving a length of yarn according to the number of stitches to be cast on, then make a slip knot, and put this onto the Needle.

Loop the long thread of yarn hanging from the knot over your left thumb. Hold the needle in your right hand with the yarn coming from ball of wool at the back. Loop this over your right hand index and third finger as shown in the illustration. Insert the point of the needle into the loop, wrap the wool in your right hand once round the needle and draw a loop through, so you now have two loops on the needle. Pull the thread quite tight. Repeat for the number of stitches required.

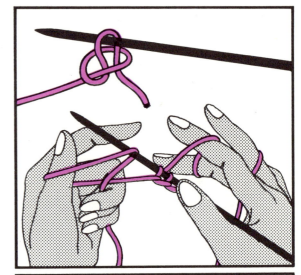

HOW TO DO PLAIN OR KNIT STITCH

Cast on required number of stitches. Hold the Needle with the cast on stitches in the left hand, with the point approximately $\frac{1}{2}$ in. above the thumb and first finger. With the other Needle in the right hand, insert the point from left to right through the first loop, pass the yarn, which in plain knitting is always at the back of the work, round the point of the right hand Needle and draw a loop through. Keep this loop on the right hand Needle, and let the old stitch slide off the left hand Needle.

Continue to the end of the row. For the next row, turn the knitting round and pass the empty Needle back into the right hand.

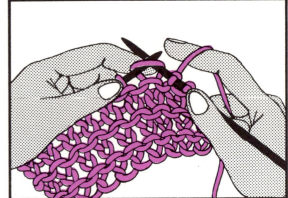

HOW TO DO PURL STITCH

Cast on. Hold the Needle with the cast on stitches in the left hand, as for Knit stitch, but keep the yarn always to the front of the work. Insert the right hand Needle from right to left through the first loop to the front instead of the back as in the Knit stitch. Now pass the yarn round the point of the Needle and draw a loop through. Keep this loop on the right hand Needle, and let the old stitch slide off the left hand Needle. Continue to the end of the row. Turn knitting round, and pass the empty needle into the right hand.

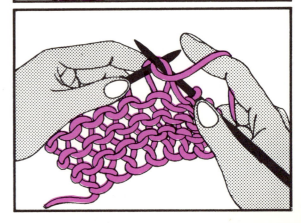

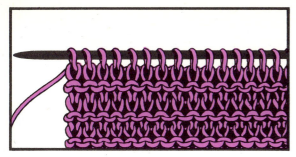

GARTER STITCH
This consists of 'Knit' rows throughout.

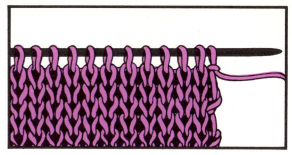

STOCKING STITCH
This consists of one Knit row and one Purl row worked alternately. The Knit side is generally considered the right side.

RIBBING
Ribbing consists of Knit and Purl stitches worked alternately in the same row, and produces a very elastic fabric for cuffs, welts, and neckbands, etc. The type of rib required for each pattern is always stated, e.g. K.2, p.2 rib means 2 Knit stitches, followed by 2 Purl stitches, all along the row.

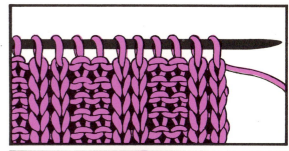

HOW TO DECREASE
To decrease 1 stitch at the beginning of a row: Slip 1 stitch, k. 1 stitch, pass the slipped stitch over the knitted stitch.
To decrease 1 stitch at the end of a row: Knit the last 2 stitches together.
For Purl, follow the same instructions, reading Purl instead of Knit.

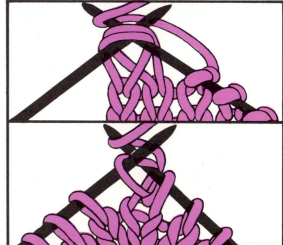

HOW TO INCREASE
Knit or Purl into the stitch, and before slipping it off the Needle, knit or purl again into the back of the loop.

CASTING OFF
Generally, the cast off row in S.S. is a knit row, but where it is a purl row, read p. for k. in the following instructions:
Knit the first 2 sts., * slip the first st. over the second, leaving 1 st. on the right hand Needle. Knit the next st., then repeat from * until 1 st. remains. Break the yarn, and draw the end right through the loop.
When working a pattern, always cast off in the pattern. This is particularly important for ribbing, or the edge may break in wear.

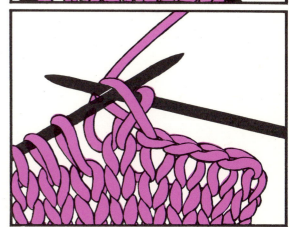

GENERAL POINTS

When it is necessary to begin a new ball of wool in knitting, it should always be joined at the end of the row. Leave a small length of the new ball of wool at the side and hold on to it as you knit the first few stitches of the row to ensure they are tightly knitted. When you have knitted back across this row, pull both ends of wool tightly again.

When knitting is finished, thread loose ends on to a darning needle and secure them by taking half a dozen or so small oversewing stitches along the outside of the work.

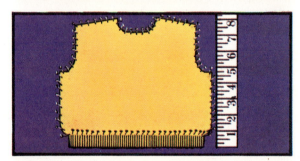

When all pieces are knitted, pin them out on an ironing board or table for pressing. Place the pins approximately $\frac{1}{2}$ in. apart and pin the work to the correct measurement. It is not necessary to pin out the ribbing and ribbing areas should never be pressed as it flattens them.

To press the knitting, steam each piece carefully by using a hot iron over a damp cloth. Do not put pressure on to the knitting, thus allowing the steam to penetrate, and do not remove the pins until each piece has cooled. If you have knitted with synthetic yarns, press with a cool iron and a dry cloth only and always follow the yarn manufacturer's instructions for washing and pressing.

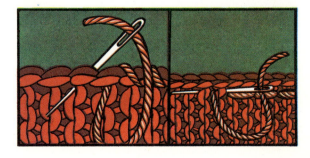

Sew each piece together with small back stitches and do not pull too tightly as you sew or the seams will be puckered. Press the seams carefully in the same way as you did the individual pieces.

Always knit a tension square before beginning a garment to check you can obtain the stated stitches and rows per inch. Instructions for this are given below.

HOW TO CHECK TENSION
Using the yarn and size of Needles stated in the instructions, work a piece of fabric not less than 3 inches square in the appropriate stitch. Carefully measure the stitches and rows to the inch.

As the work of individual knitters varies in tightness, you may find that you cannot obtain the correct row tension, even though the stitches are correct. This does not matter in most cases, as most knitting instructions are based on measurement in inches, rather than stating a certain number of rows to be worked. However, if a certain number of rows is specified, and you know that you did not obtain the correct row tension on your test piece, you must note the difference between the two tensions, and adjust the rows you knit accordingly, either by subtracting rows if you have fewer rows to the inch, or adding rows if you have more. E.g. Suppose the row tension stated is 8 rows to the inch, and the instructions state work 24 rows, then the work will measure 3 in. long. If, for instance, you have only 6 rows to the inch, and you work 24 rows, your work will measure 4 in. Therefore, you must subtract 1 in. (6 rows), in order to obtain the correct measurement. If, on the other hand, you have 10 rows to the inch, and you work 24 rows, your work will measure approximately $2\frac{1}{2}$ in. Therefore, you must add $\frac{1}{2}$ in. (5 rows), in order to obtain the correct measurement.

It is essential to obtain the correct number of stitches to the inch. A size smaller or larger Needle than that stated may be used to adjust this; smaller Needles will give you more stitches to the inch, and larger Needles will give you fewer.

ABBREVIATIONS
The following abbreviations are used commonly in knitting patterns.

K	= Knit (plain stitch)	n.r.	= Next Row
P	= Purl	sts	= stitches
SS	= Stocking Stitch	inc	= Increase stitches
G.S.	= Garter Stitch	dec	= Decrease stitches
r	= Row	tog	= Together (as in K2 sts tog.)
		F.I.	= Fair Isle
		beg.	= Beginning

CROCHET
We have used crochet to trim some of our knitted garments, and specific instructions for working this are given below. First of all however, we give instructions for making a chain, which is the equivalent of casting on in knitting.

TO WORK A CHAIN
Fold yarn (close to the end) into a loop. Using the crochet hook pull yarn through to make a slip knot and leave this loop on the hook. Hold the crochet hook between the thumb and index finger of your right hand. Hold yarn or chain between thumb and second finger of your left hand and loop the wool over the index finger of your left hand. You can then use the crochet hook to twist round the wool. (Reverse all instructions if you are left handed).
Holding the yarn and hook as described, with one loop on

the hook, twist yarn round hook once. Hold base of slip knot with left hand as described and pull hook with yarn through the loop on the hook to make a new one. Repeat this procedure until work is required length. (The illustration on the right shows a close-up of the first stitch being worked in a chain.)

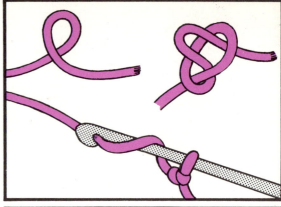

TO MAKE A DOUBLE CROCHET EDGING

Hold the knitting horizontally with the right side facing you. Crochet will be worked from right to left, one whole knitted st. away from the edge. (Left-handed people work from left to right). Knot the crochet yarn to the appropriate edge of knitting. Insert the hook, from the front, through first st. of knitting, one whole st. away from the edge (i.e. under the two top threads), and pick up crochet yarn. You should now have 1 loop on hook.

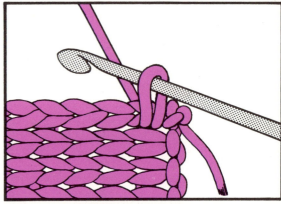

2. Insert hook from the front under the two top strands of the first knitted st. Catch yarn with hook. (This is known as "thread over".) Draw yarn through knitted fabric. (2 loops on hook).

3. Thread over hook and draw through 2 loops on hook —1 loop remains on hook. This completes 1 double crochet st.

4. To make next double crochet st., insert hook from the front under the two top strands of the next knitted st. Thread over hook. Now continue working along the knitted edge, repeating steps 3 to 5 throughout.

GENERAL POINTS

It is not always necessary to work 1 double crochet st. into every knitted st. This depends on the thickness of the knitting yarn, but the important thing is always to keep the work flat, so space the crochet sts. accordingly, and if it is necessary to miss spaces, miss them evenly along the crochet r. If you work too many crochet sts., the knitting will stretch, and if you work too few, it will gather.

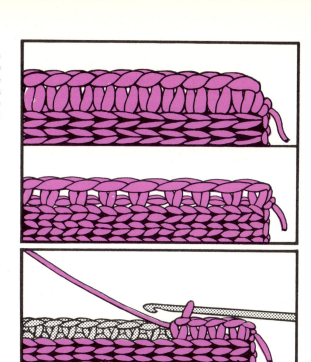

When you are working round a back opening, or along 2 front edges, they must match together. When you come to the second edge, pin it to the first edge as you work, to ensure a good match.

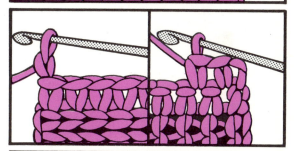

If 2 rs. of double crochet are specified in the instructions, when you reach the end of the first r., work 1 chain st. (simply thread over hook and draw through loop already on hook). Turn the work, so that the reverse faces you, and begin another r. of double crochet sts., working into the spaces formed by the first r.

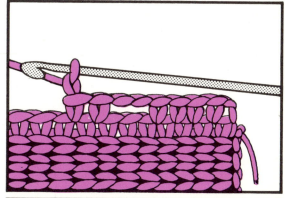

Where button loops are required, work these in chain st. (the number of chains depending on the size of the buttons). Work the button loops at even intervals during the second r. of double crochet, missing the appropriate number of double crochet spaces in the first r. before re-starting double crochet. Remember that loops of wool tend to stretch, so do not make them too large, or the garment will gape in wear.

When joining 2 knitted pieces together with double crochet, hold the pieces with wrong sides together, and work crochet through both layers at once.

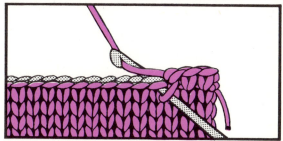

Baby's Hooded Cape

Just the thing to keep baby snug and warm on blowy days. This all-in-one cape and hood fits a baby—approximately 6 months old.

TENSION:
7 sts. and 9 rs. to 1 inch, knitting S.S. on no. 10 ns.

YOU WILL NEED:
4 50grm balls 4 ply Courtelle Crepe in main colour (white)
1 50grm ball in contrast colour (pink)
Oddment of Green for embroidery
No. 10 and No. 12 Knitting needles
Size 2.50 crochet hook
4 stitch holders.

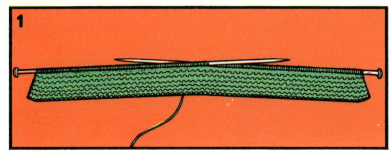

1

Using contrast colour, and No. 10 Ns, cast on 136 sts. Work 2 rs. G.S. *nr:* * K.2 k.2 tog., K to last 4 sts. K.2 tog, K.2. *nr:* K * Repeat from * to * 3 times. (See page 77 for abbreviations).

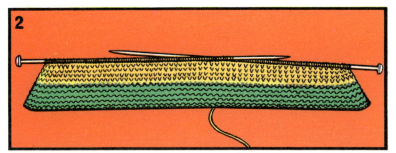

2

Change to main colour, and work in S.S. beg. with a K.r K.2 K.2 tog., K to last 4 sts. K.2 tog., K.2.*nr:* P.

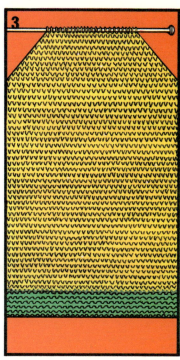

3

Repeat last 2 rs until 24 sts remain, ending with a P.r.

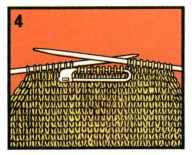

4

Shape neck—K.2, K.2 tog., K.4. Slip next 8 sts onto holder. Slip remaining 8 sts onto spare N.

5

nr: Cast off 2 sts at inner edge. P. to end. *nr:* K.2, K.2 tog. K to end. *nr:* as first row. *nr:* K.1, K.2 tog. Cast off.

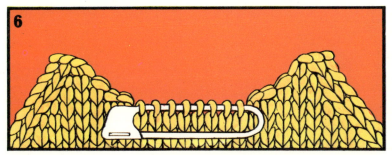

6

Rejoin wool to inner end of sts on spare N. with R.S. facing *nr:* Cast off 2 sts, K. to end. *nr:* P.2, P.2 together, P to end. *nr:* as first r. *nr:* P.1 P.2 tog. Cast off remaining 2 sts.

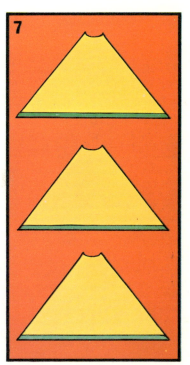

7

Work 3 more panels in the same way.

PATTERN FOR CAPE AND HOOD

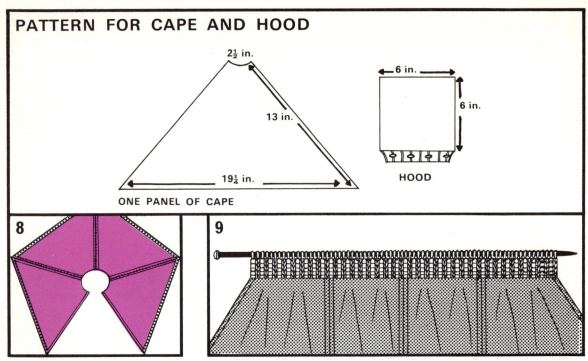

2½ in.

13 in.

19¼ in.

ONE PANEL OF CAPE

6 in.

6 in.

HOOD

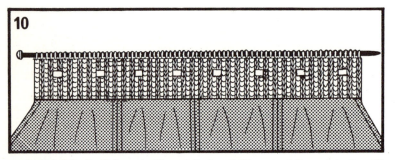

8

Neckband—Join 3 side seams leaving 4th seam open.

9

Using No. 12 Ns and main colour, with W.S. of work facing, pick up 72 sts, (including sts from holder). Work 4 rs K.1 P.1 rib.

10

nr: in K.1 P.1 rib, K.2 cast off next 2 sts., K.7*, repeat from * to * until 5 sts remain. Cast off next 2 sts. K.3 (8 holes). nr: in rib, K.3* cast on 2 sts. K.7* Repeat from * to * until 4 sts remain. Cast on 2 sts. K.2 Work 2 rs in rib.

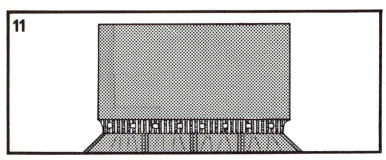

11

Hood—Change to No. 10 Ns and in S.S. K.2*. Inc. into next st., K.5*. Repeat from * to * 10 more times. Inc. into next st. K.3 (84 sts). Work 55 rs in S.S. Cast off.

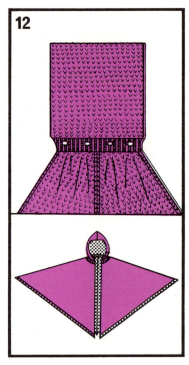

12

Fold hood in half and join top seam.

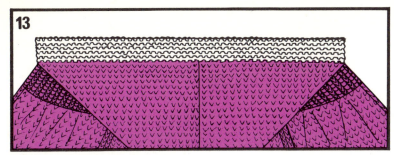

Hood Edging: In contrast colour and No. 10 ns., right side facing, pick up 72 sts along front edge of hood between upper edges of ribbed neckband. Work 10 rs G.S. Cast off.

Fold back G.S. rs. along edge of hood and catch down. Join front seam of cape to within 4 in. of base of neckband.

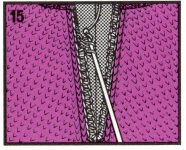

With 2.50 crochet hook and main colour, work 1r double crochet round neck opening.

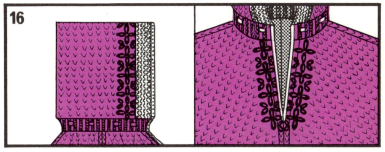

Embroider lazy daisy st. flowers round hood and front opening.

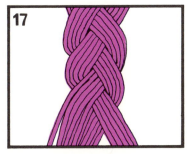

Neck cord—cut 15 strands of main colour yarn, about 1 yd long, and plait together in 3 groups of 5 strands.

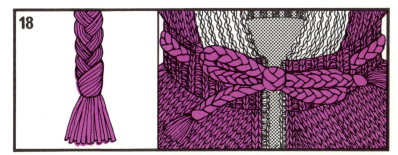

Knot ends and trim tassels. Thread cord through neckband holes and tie.

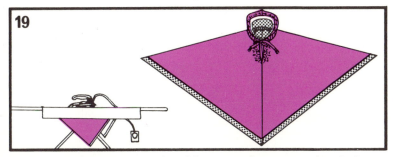

Press finished garment gently with a warm iron over a dry cloth.

Knitted Popover Dress

This delightful little popover dress is very easy to make and quite enchanting to look at.

MEASUREMENTS:
Our pattern fits a child of 9 months (1 year, 18 months) — chest sizes 19 (19½, 20) inches. Figures in brackets refer to larger sizes respectively.

YOU WILL NEED:
3(3, 4) 50 grm balls of 4 ply wool in main colour (Turquoise)
1 50 grm ball 4 ply wool in each of 3 contrasting colours (Royal Blue, White and Yellow)
No. 8, No. 10 and No. 12 Knitting Needles
Size 2.50 crochet hook
Stitch holder
3 small buttons
Flower motif

1 BACK—Using No. 8 Ns. cast on 118(120, 124)sts. Begin with a K.r. and work 6 rs in S.S. Change to No. 10 Ns. and continue until work measures 8(8½, 9) in. from cast-on edge, ending with a P.r.

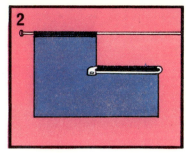

2 Back opening—K. 59(60, 62)sts. Put remaining sts on holder. Turn, knit 2in. ending with a K.r.—[59(60, 62)sts.].

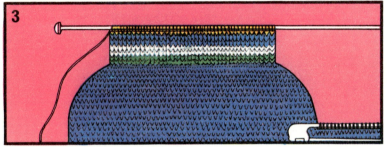

3 ** P.2 tog., *P.2 tog., P.1* Repeat from * to * until 0(1, 3)sts remain on needle. P. to end 39(40, 42)sts. *Bodice*—work S.S. in 2r stripes using 3 colours and main colour. K.6rs. (You will need to work 1r extra here on other side of bodice.)

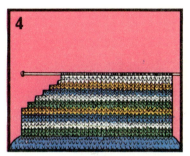

4 Shape armhole—* cast off 2 sts at beg. of next r. P.1 r.* Repeat from * to * 4(4,5) more times. Dec 1st at beg. of next r.

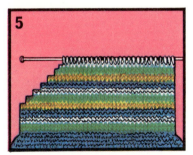

5 *1st and 2nd sizes only*—P. 1r Dec 1 st at beg of next row. All sizes—27(28, 29)sts. remain.

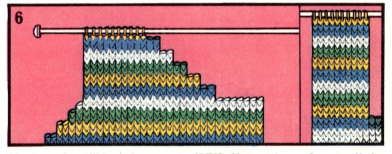

6 Shape neck—still in stripes, cast off 7(8, 9)sts at beg. of next r. K. 1r. *Cast off 2 sts at beg of next r. K.1r* Repeat from * to * 4 more times (10sts remain). Work 4¼(4¾, 5¼) in. from beg of armhole shaping ending with a P.r.

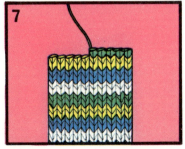

7 Shape shoulder—cast off 5 sts at beg of next r. Cast off remaining 5 sts.**

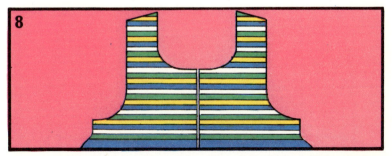

8 Pick up 59(60, 62) sts from holder. With R.S. facing rejoin wool to inner end of stitches. Work 2 in. ending with a K.r. Follow instructions from ** to **, noting extra r. to be worked before armhole shaping.

Front—using main colour and No. 8 Ns. cast on 118(120, 124) sts. Starting with K.r., work 6 rs. S.S. Change to No. 10 Ns and continue until work measures 10(10½, 11) in. from cast-on edge, ending with a K.r.

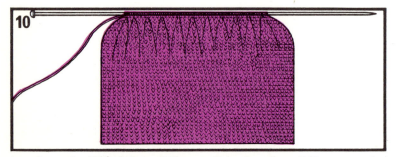

1st size only—*P.1, P.2 tog.* Repeat from * to * until 4 sts remain. P.2 together twice (78sts). *2nd size*—* P.1. P.2 tog.* Repeat from * to * to end (80sts). *3rd size*—P.2,* P.1, P.2 tog.* Repeat from * to * until 2sts remain. P.2 (84sts).

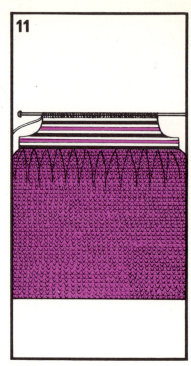

Bodice (stripes as back) K. 6rs. *Shape armholes*—cast off 2sts. at beg of next 10(10, 12)rs. Dec 1 at beg of next 4(4, 2)rs.

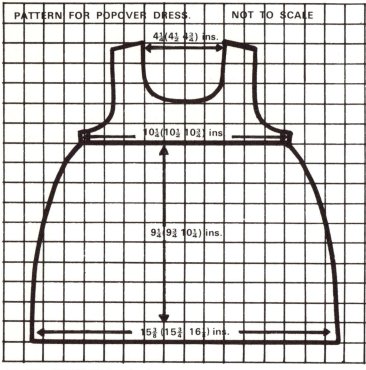

PATTERN FOR POPOVER DRESS.   NOT TO SCALE

4¼(4½ 4¾) ins.

10¼(10½ 10¾) ins

9¼(9¾ 10¼) ins.

15⅜(15¾ 16¼) ins.

To FIT a 19(19½ 20) in. chest

Diagram shows shape of dress. It is not drawn to scale.

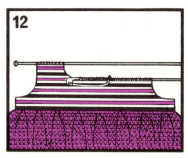

K. 20sts., put 14(16, 18)sts. on to holder. Put 20sts on to spare N. Turn, * cast off 2sts. K.1r.* Repeat from * to * 4 more times (10sts.).

Continue until work is 4¼(4¾, 5¼)in. from armhole shaping (end with P.r.) Cast off 5sts at beg of nr. K to end. Cast off.

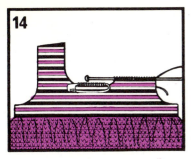

Pick up 20sts from spare N. Rejoin wool at outer end of W.S. P.1r. Cast off 2sts at beg of next r. P.1r.

Repeat from * to * 4 more times (10sts remain). Continue until work measures $4\frac{1}{4}(4\frac{3}{4}, 5\frac{1}{4})$in. from armhole shaping, ending with a K.r. Cast off 5sts at beg. of next r. P. to end. Cast off remaining 5sts.

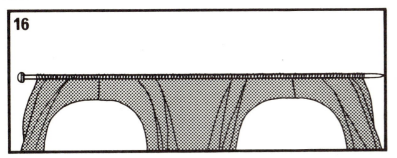

Neckband—pin out each piece to size and press (see page 76). Take care not to press gathers flat. Join shoulder seams. Press. Using No. 12ns and main colour, R.S. facing, pick up 118(122, 126)sts round neckline (including sts. from holder).

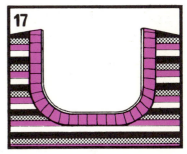

Work 6 rs of K.2, P.2 rib. Cast off in rib.

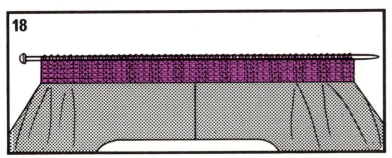

Armhole bands—(both alike). Using No. 12 Ns and main colour, R.S. facing, pick up 52(56, 60)sts round armhole. Work 6 rs of K.2, P.2, rib. Cast off in rib.

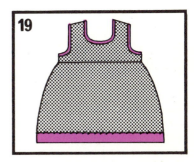

Join side seams. Press. Fold 6 rs round lower edge to W.S. and catch down using cotton thread. Press carefully.

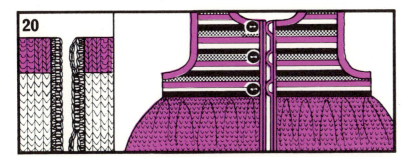

Using main colour wool and size 2.50 crochet hook, work 2 rs double crochet round back opening. Include 3 chain st. button loops within striped section on right side edge in second row (see page 79). Sew on 3 buttons to correspond.

Sew motif into position and give a final light press.

Fair Isle for All

Fair Isle knitting looks so impressive, and it really is not so difficult to do. Follow our instructions to make these super garments—a trendy little tank top and a zip-up cardigan. Suitable for boys or girls, they are bound to be winners with all youngsters. (If Fair Isle knitting still seems a little too ambitious, follow the instructions for making the tank top in just one colour.)

MEASUREMENTS (for tank top):
To fit a child of approximately 5(6, 7) years—chest sizes 23(24, 25) inches. For garment measurements, see diagram.

TENSION (for tank top):
7½ sts. and 9 rs. to 1 inch, knitting S.S. on No. 10 Needles.

YOU WILL NEED
(for tank top):
2(2, 3) 50 grm. balls 4 ply wool in main colour (Yellow)
1 50 grm. ball 4 ply wool in contrast colour (Green)
A pair each of No. 12, No. 10, and No. 9 Knitting Needles.
N.B. For a plain top, omit contrast wool and No. 9 Knitting Needles.

BACK AND FRONT (both alike):
Using YELLOW wool and No. 12 Ns., cast on 86(90, 94) sts. Work 1½ inches of K.2, P.2 rib, increasing 6(5, 5) sts. evenly across the work in the last r. (92(95, 99) sts. altogether).
Change to No. 10 Ns. and S.S., and starting with a K. r., work 4 rs.
Change to No. 9 Ns. and using YELLOW (Y) and GREEN (G), work 29 rs. of Fair Isle as follows:

FAIR ISLE TOP ONLY:
(for plain top continue in S.S. for 29 rs. in ONE colour only)
1st r: K.2(3,5)Y, *3G, 1Y. Repeat from * until 2(4,6) sts. remain. K. Y to end.
2nd r: P.4(6,8)Y, *1G, 3Y. Repeat from * until 0(1,2) sts. remain. P.Y to end.
3rd r: K.5(6,8)Y, *1G, 3Y. Repeat from * until 3(5,7) sts remain. K.Y to end.
4th r: P.1(3,5)Y, 1G, 3Y, *3G, 1Y. Repeat from * until 3(4,6) sts. remain. P.1Y, 1G. P.Y to end.
5th r: K.1(2,4)Y, 2G. K.Y until 3(5,7) sts. remain. K.2G, K.Y to end.
6th r: P.1(3,5)Y, 1G, 2Y, 1G. P.Y until 5(6,8) sts. remain. P. 1G, 2Y, 1G. P.Y to end.
7th r: K.3(4,6)Y, 2G, 1Y, 2G, 3Y, 1G, 3Y, 1G, 23Y, 2G, 3Y, 1G, 3Y, 1G, 23Y, 2G, 3Y, 1G, 3Y, 1G, 5Y, 2G, K. Y to end.
8th r: P.1(3,5)Y, 1G, 2Y, 1G, 6Y, 1G, 2Y, 2G, 3Y, 1G, 9Y, 1G, 14Y, 1G, 2Y, 2G, 3Y, 1G, 9Y, 1G, 14Y, 1G, 2Y, 2G, 3Y, 1G, 1Y, 1G, 2Y, 1G, P, Y to end.
9th r: K1(2,4)Y, 2G, 3Y, 1G, 2Y, 1G, 1Y, 1G, 2Y, 1G, 13Y, 3G, 8Y, 1G, 2Y, 1G, 1Y, 1G, 2Y, 1G, 13Y, 3G, 8Y, 1G, 2Y, 1G, 1Y, 1G, 2Y, 1G, 8Y, 2G, K. Y to end.
10th r: P.1(3,5)Y, 1G, 2Y, 1G, 6Y, 1G, 1Y, 1G, 3Y, 3G, 4Y, 2G, 2Y, 3G, 2Y, 2G, 9Y, 1G, 1Y, 1G, 3Y, 3G, 4Y, 2G, 2Y, 3G, 2Y, 2G, 9Y, 1G, 1Y, 1G, 3Y, 3G, 1Y, 1G, 2Y,

1G, P. Y to end.
11th r: K.3(4,6)Y, 2G, 2Y, 2G, 4Y, 2G, 9Y, 2G, 3Y, 1G, 3Y, 2G, 5Y, 2G, 4Y, 2G, 9Y, 2G, 3Y, 1G, 3Y, 2G, 5Y, 2G, 4Y, 2G, 6Y, 2G, K. Y to end.
12th r: P.1(3,5)Y, 1G, 2Y, 1G, 5Y, 9G, 7Y, 1G, 2Y, 1G, 2Y, 1G, 10Y, 9G, 7Y, 1G, 2Y, 1G, 2Y, 1G, 10Y, 9G, 2Y, 1G, 2Y, 1G. P. Y to end.
13th r: K.1(2,4)Y, 2G, 3Y, 10G, 11Y, 1G, 1Y, 1G, 1Y, 1G, 7Y, 10G, 11Y, 1G, 1Y, 1G, 1Y, 1G, 7Y, 10G, 7Y, 2G, K. Y to end.
14th r: P.1(3,5)Y, 1G, 2Y, 1G, 4Y, 11G, 3Y, 2G, 3Y, 1G, 1Y, 1G, 3Y, 2G, 6Y, 11G, 3Y, 2G, 3Y, 1G, 1Y, 1G, 3Y, 2G, 6Y, 11G, 1Y, 1G, 2Y, 1G, P. Y to end.
15th r: K.3(4,6)Y, 2G, 2Y, 10G, 5Y, 6G, 1Y, 1G, 1Y, 6G, 3Y, 10G, 5Y, 6G, 1Y, 1G, 1Y, 6G, 3Y, 10G, 4Y, 2G, K. Y to end.
16th r: P.1(3,5)Y, 1G, 2Y, 1G, 4Y, 4G, 10Y, 2G, 3Y, 1G, 1Y, 1G, 3Y, 2G, 6Y, 4G, 10Y, 2G, 3Y, 1G, 1Y, 1G, 3Y, 2G, 6Y, 4G, 8Y, 1G, 2Y, 1G, P. Y to end.
17th r: K.1(2,4)Y, 2G, 12Y, 5G, 7Y, 1G, 1Y, 1G, 1Y, 1G, 16Y, 5G, 7Y, 1G, 1Y, 1G, 1Y, 1G, 16Y, 5G, 3Y, 2G, K. Y to end.
18th r: P.1(3,5)Y, 1G, 2Y, 1G, 2Y, 3G, 16Y, 1G, 2Y, 1G, 2Y, 1G, 7Y, 3G, 16Y, 1G, 2Y, 1G, 2Y, 1G, 7Y, 3G, 11Y, 1G, 2Y, 1G, P. Y to end.
19th r: K.3(4,6)Y, 2G, 5Y, 3G, 1Y, 2G, 1Y, 1G, 6Y, 2G, 3Y, 1G, 3Y, 2G, 8Y, 3G, 1Y, 2G, 1Y, 1G, 6Y, 2G, 3Y, 1G, 3Y, 2G, 8Y, 3G, 1Y, 2G, 1Y, 1G, 3Y, 2G, K. Y to end.
20th r: P.1(3,5)Y, 1G, 2Y, 1G, 4Y, 1G, 2Y, 1G, 3Y, 1G, 7Y, 2G, 2Y, 3G, 2Y, 2G, 7Y, 1G, 2Y, 1G, 3Y, 1G, 7Y, 2G, 2Y, 3G, 2Y, 2G, 7Y, 1G, 2Y, 1G, 3Y, 1G, 4Y, 1G, 2Y, 1G, P. Y to end.
21st r: K.1(2,4)Y, 2G, 6Y, 1G, 2Y, 1G, 3Y, 1G, 2Y, 1G, 8Y, 3G, 11Y, 1G, 2Y, 1G, 3Y, 1G, 2Y, 1G, 8Y, 3G, 11Y, 1G, 2Y, 1G, 3Y, 1G, 2Y, 1G,

3Y, 2G, K. Y to end.
22nd r: P.1(3,5)Y, 1G, 2Y, 1G, 2Y, 2G, 4Y, 1G, 15Y, 1G, 10Y, 2G, 4Y, 1G, 15Y, 1G, 10Y, 2G, 4Y, 1G, 7Y, 1G, 2Y, 1G, P. Y to end.
23rd r: K3(4,6)Y, 2G, 14Y, 1G, 32Y, 1G, 32Y, 1G, 1Y, 2G, K. Y to end.
24th r: As 6th r.
25th r: As 5th r.
26th r: As 4th r.
27th r: As 3rd r.
28th r: As 2nd r.
29th r: As 1st r.

BOTH TOPS:
Change to No. 10 Ns., and starting with a P. r., work S.S. until work measures 8(8¼,8½) inches from cast on edge, ending with a K. r.

Next r: Dec. 6(5,5) sts. evenly across the work. (86(90,94) sts. remain). Change to No. 12 Ns., and work 5 rs. of K.2, P.2 rib. Cast off in rib.

RIGHT SHOULDER STRAP:
Using yellow wool and No. 12 Ns., cast on 86(90,94) sts. and work 5 rs. K.2, P.2 rib.
Change to No. 10 Ns. and S.S., and starting with a K.R., work as follows:
1st r: K.43(45,47), K.2 together, K to end.
2nd r: P.42(44,46), P.2 together, P to end.
3rd r: K.42(44,46), K.2 together, K. to end.
4th r: P.41(43,45), P.2 together, P. to end.
(82(86,90) sts. remain). Change to No. 12 Ns. and work 5 rs. K.2, P.2 rib. Cast off in rib.

LEFT SHOULDER STRAP:
Follow the instructions for Right Shoulder Strap, but read P for K. and vice versa, throughout.

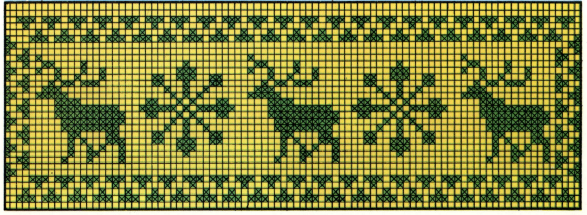

TO MAKE UP: Pin out each piece to size and press. Join side seams; press.

Plain Top only: Change to No. 10 Ns. and S.S. and starting with a K. r, continue until work measures $8(8\frac{1}{4}, 8\frac{1}{2})$ in. from cast-on edge, ending with a K. r.

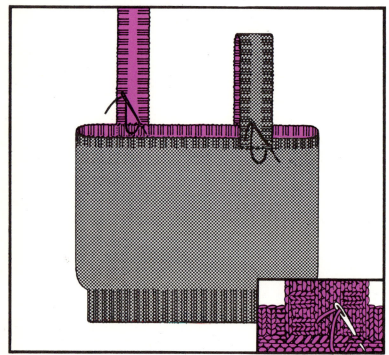

Fold straps in half and pin each end into position approximately 2 in. in from side seams, with the ends of the straps inside. Catch down the ends of the straps to the first r. of top ribbing. Give final light press.

Zip Jacket

MEASUREMENTS:
To fit a child of approximately 5(6, 7) years—chest sizes 23(24,25) inches. For garment measurements, see diagram.

TENSION:
$7\frac{1}{2}$ sts. and 9 rs. to 1 inch, knitting S.S. on No. 10 Ns.

BACK:
Using WHITE wool and No. 12 Ns., cast on 90(94,98) sts. and work $1\frac{1}{2}$ inches of K.2, P.2 rib, increasing 5 sts. evenly across the work in the last r. 95(99,103) sts. altogether.
Change to No. 10 Ns., and, starting with a K. r., work in S.S. until Back measures 4(4,5) inches from cast-on edge, ending with a P. r.
Work 28 rs. of Fair Isle as follows:
1st r: K.4(6,8)W, *3R, 9W. Repeat from * until 7(9,11) sts. remain. K.3 R, K. W to end.
2nd r: As 1st r, but read P. for K.
3rd r: As 1st r.
4th r: P. W throughout.
5th r: K. W throughout.
6th r: P. 1(3,0)R, 9(9,2)W, *3R, 9W. Repeat from * until 1(3,5) sts. remain. P.1(3,3)R. 3rd size only: P. W to end.
7th r: As 6th r., but read K. for P.
8th r: As 6th r.
9th r: K.5(7,9)W, *1G, 11W. Repeat from * until 6(8,10) sts. remain. K. 1G, K. W to end.
10th r: P.4(6,8)W, * 3G, 9W. Repeat from * until 7(9,11) sts. remain. P.3G, P. W to end.
11th r: K.3(5,7)W, *5G, 7W. Repeat from * until 8(10,12) sts. remain. K.5G, K.W to end.
12th r: P.2(4,0)W, 7(7,1)G, *5W, 7G. Repeat from * until 2(4,6) sts. remain. P.2(4,5)W.
3rd size only: P.G to end.
13th r: K.1(2,0)W.
3rd size only: K.2G, 3W.
All sizes: *K.4G, 1R, 4G, 3W. Repeat from * until 10(12,14) sts. remain. K.4G, 1R, 4G, 1(3,3)W.
3rd size only: K.G to end.
14th r : P.4(1,3)G.
2nd and 3rd sizes only: P.1W, 4G.
All sizes: *P.3R, 4G, 1W, 4G. Repeat from * until 7(9,11) sts. remain. P.3R, 4G.
2nd and 3rd sizes only: P.1W, P.6 to end.
15th r: K.3(5,7)G, * 5R, 7G. Repeat from * until 8(10,12) sts. remain. K.5R, K.G to end.
16th r: P.2(4,0)G, 7(7,1)R, *5G, 7R. Repeat from * until 2(4,6) sts. remain. P.2(4,5)G.
3rd size only: P.R to end.
17th r: K.1(3,0)G, 9(9,2)R, *3G, 9R. Repeat from * until 1(3,5) sts. remain. K.1(3,3)G.

3rd size only: K.R to end.
18th r: P.1(1,3)R, *1G, 11R. Repeat from * until 0(2,4) sts. remain. P.1G, P.R to end.
**19th r: As 18th r, but read K. for P.
20th r: As 17th r, but read P. for K.
21st r: As 16th r, but read K. for P.
22nd r: As 15th r, but read P. for K.
23rd r: As 14th r, but read K. for P.
24th r: As 13th r, but read P. for K.
25th r: As 12th r, but read K. for P.
26th r: As 11th r, but read P. for K.
27th r: As 10th r, but read K. for P.
28th r: As 9th r, but read P. for K.**
Continue in S.S., using WHITE only, until work measures $7\frac{3}{4}(7\frac{3}{4},8\frac{3}{4})$ inches from cast-on edge. Cast off.

FRONTS (2 alike):
Using WHITE wool and No. 12 Ns., cast on 44(46,46) sts. and work $1\frac{1}{2}$ inches of K.2, P.2 rib, increasing 3(3,5) sts. evenly across the work in the last r. 47(49, 51) sts. altogether.
Change to No. 10 Ns. and, starting with a K.R, work in S.S. until Front measures 4(4,5) inches from cast-on edge, ending with a P.R. Work 28 rs. of Fair Isle as follows:
1st r : K.4(5,6)W, *3R, 9W. Repeat from * until 7(8,9) sts. remain. K.3R, K.W to end.
2nd R: As 1st r, but read P. for K.
3rd r: As 1st r.
4th r: P.W throughout.
5th r: K.W throughout.
6th r: P.1(2,3)R, *9W, 3R. Repeat from * until 10(11, 12) sts remain. P.9W, P.R to end.
7th r: As 6th R, but read K. for P.
8th r: As 6th R.
9th r: K.5(6,7)W, *1G, 11W. Repeat from * until 6(7,8) sts. remain. K.1G, K.W to end.
10th r: P.4(5,6)W, *3G, 9W. Repeat from * until 7(8,9) sts. remain. P.3G, P.W to end.
11th r: K.3(4,5)W, *5G, 7W. Repeat from * until 8(9, 10) sts. remain. K.5G, K.W to end.
12th r: P.2(3,4)W, *7G, 5W. Repeat from * until 9(10,11) sts. remain. P.7G, P.W to end.
13th r: K.1(2,3)W, *4G, 1R, 4G, 3W. Repeat from * until 10(11, 12) sts. remain. K.4G, 1R, 4G. K.W to end.
14th r: 2nd and 3rd sizes only: P(1,0)W, (0,1)G, (0,1)W. All sizes: *P.4G, 3R, 4G, 1W. Repeat from *

until 11(12,13) sts. remain. P.4G, 3R, 4G.
2nd and 3rd sizes only: P.1W, (0,1)G.
15th r: K.3(4,5)G, *5R, 7G. Repeat from * until 8(9,10) sts. remain. K.5R, K.G to end.
16th r: P.2(3,4)G, *7R, 5G. Repeat from * until 9(10,11) sts. remain. P.7R, P.G to end.
17th r: K.1(2,3)G, *9R, 3G. Repeat from * until 10(11,12) sts. remain. K.9R, K. G to end.
18th r: P.0(1,0)G, 11(11,1)R, *1G, 11R. Repeat from * until 0(1,2) sts. remain. P.0(1,1)G, 0(0,1)R.
Now follow instructions for Back from ** to the end.

SLEEVES and YOKE (1 piece):
Using WHITE wool and No. 12 Ns. cast on 42(46,50) sts., and work $1\frac{1}{2}$ inches of K.2, P.2 rib, increasing 7 sts. evenly across the work in the last r. (49(53, 57) sts. altogether.)
Change to No. 10 Ns. and, starting with a K.R., work in S.S. Work 2 rs. Increase 1 st. at both ends of the next and every following 4th(6th, 3rd) r., until the 19th(17th,32nd) increase R. has been worked and there are 87(87,121) sts. Work another 19(5,18) rs. in S.S.
(Work measures 12(13,14) inches from cast on edge.) (Adjust sleeve length at this stage if desired, but always end with a P.r.) Work 28 rs. of Fair Isle as follows:
***1st r: K.0(0,5)W, *3R, 9W. Repeat from * until 3(3,8) sts. remain. K.3R, 0(0,5)W.
2nd r: As 1st R., but read P. for K.
3rd r: As 1st r.
4th r: P.W. throughout.
5th r: K.W throughout.
6th r: P.6(6,0)W, 3(3,2)R, *9W, 3R. Repeat from * until 6(6,11) sts. remain. P.6(6,9)W, 0(0,2)R.
7th r: As 6th r., but read K. for P.
8th r: As 6th r.
9th r: K.1(1,6)W, *1G, 11W. Repeat from * until 2(2,7) sts. remain. K.1G, K.W to end.

10th r: P.0(0,5)W, *3G, 9W. Repeat from * until 3(3,8) sts. remain. P.3G, P.W to end.

11th r: K.0(0,4)W, 4(4,5)G, *7W, 5G. Repeat from * until 11(11,4) sts. remain. K.7(7,4)W, 4(4,0)G.

12th r: P'0(0,3)W, 5(5,7)G, *5W, 7G. Repeat from * until 10(10,3) sts remain. P.5(5,3)W, 5(5,0)G.

13th r: K.1(1,0)G.
3rd size only: K.2W, 4G.
All sizes: *K.1R, 4G, 3W, 4G. Repeat from * until 2(2,7) sts remain.
1st and 2nd sizes only: K.1R, 1G.
3rd size only: K.1R, 4G. K.W to end.

14th r: P.3(3,0)R.
3rd size only: P.1W, 4G, 3R.
All sizes: *P.4G, 1W, 4G, 3R. Repeat from * until 0(0,5) sts remain. 3rd size only: P.4G, 1W.

15th r: K.4(4,0)R, 7(7,4)G, *5R, 7G. Repeat from * until 4(4,9) sts. remain. K.4(4,5)R, 0(0,4)G.

16th r: P.5(5,0)R, 5(5,3)G, *7R, 5G. Repeat from * until 5(5,10) sts. remain. P.5(5,7)R, 0(0,3)G.

17th r: K.6(6,0)R, 3(3,2)G, *9R, 3G. Repeat from * until 6(6,11) sts. remain. K.6(6,9)R, 0(0,2)G.

18th r: P.7(7,0)R, *1G, 11R. Repeat from * until 8(8,1) sts. remain. P.1G, P.R to end.

Now follow instructions for Back from ** to **.   ***

Continue in S.S. using WHITE only, and work 5(5,7) rs.

Next r: P.44(44,61) sts. slip the remaining 43(43,60) sts. onto the st. holder. Turn, and work front neckline shaping as follows:

1st r: Cast off 4 sts. at the beginning. K. to end.

2nd r: P.

3rd r: As 1st r.

4th r: P.

5th r: As 1st r.

6th r: P.

7th r: Cast off 3 sts. at the beginning. K. to end.

8th r: P.

9th r: Cast off 2 sts. at the beginning. K. to end.

10th r: P.

11th r: Decrease 1 st at the beginning, K. to end.

12th r: P.

13th r: As 11th r.

14th r: P.

15th r: As 11th r.

24(24,41) sts. remain. Work a further 4(5,6) rs. Cast off.

With the wrong side of the work facing, pick up the 43(43,60) sts. from the st. holder, rejoin WHITE wool, and starting with a P. r., work 38(40,42) rs. S.S. Slip these sts. back onto the st. holder.

Using No. 10 Ns. and WHITE wool, cast on 24(24,41) sts., and starting with a K. r., work 4(6,6) rs. S.S. *Increase 1st. at the beginning of the next r. K. to end. P.1 r.* Repeat from * to * twice more.

Cast on 2 sts. at the beginning of the next r. K. to end. P.1 r.

Cast on 3 sts. at beginning of next r. K. to end. P.1r.

Cast on 4 sts. at the beginning of the next r. K. to end. P.1 r.

Repeat from * to * twice more. 44(44,61) sts. altogether.

With the wrong side of the work facing, pick up the 43(43,60) sts. from the st. holder onto the same N. as the 44(44,61) sts. Rejoin WHITE wool to outer edge of sts. from the st. holder, and starting with a K. r., work 4(4,6) rs. S.S. Now work 28 rs. of Fair Isle, following the instructions from *** to ***. Continuing in S.S., using WHITE wool only, work 20(8, 19) rs. If you adjusted the sleeve length previously, remember to make the same adjustment here.

Decrease 1 st at both ends of the next and every following 4th(6th, 3rd) r., until the 19th(17th,32nd) decrease r. has been worked, and 49(53,57) sts. remain.

Work 1 r. Decrease 7 sts. evenly across the work in the next r. 42 (46,50) sts remain.

Change to No. 12 Ns., and work 1½ inches of K.2, P.2 rib. Cast off in rib.

NECKBAND

With the wrong side of the yoke facing, and using No. 12 Ns. and WHITE wool, pick up 84(86,88) sts. evenly round the neck edge, and work 2 inches of K.2, P.2 rib. Cast off in rib.

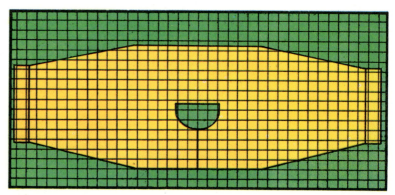

(This chart shows the shape of the yoke and sleeves which are all knitted in one piece.)

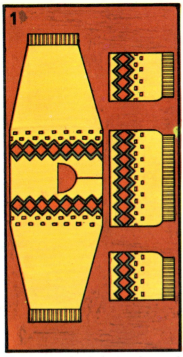

1 Pin out each piece to size and press.

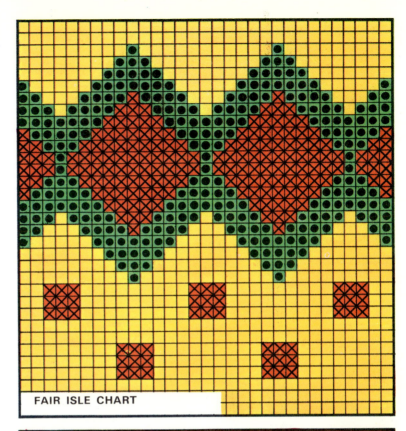

FAIR ISLE CHART

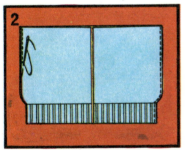

2 R.S. together, pin and sew fronts and back together along side seams.

3 R.S. inside, fold yoke and sleeves in half lengthwise. Pin the lower half of jacket in place. Sew along sleeve and yoke seams. Press.

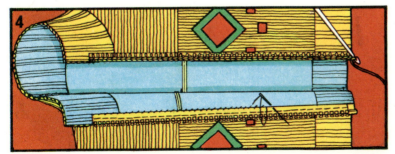

4 Using White wool and a 2.50 crochet hook, work 2 rows of double crochet (see page 78) along both front edges, including neckband edges. Press. Backstitch zip in place.

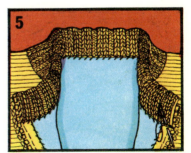

5 Fold neck band in half lengthwise and catch cast-off edge down neatly on inside. Give a final light press.

Fair Isle Mittens

These mittens will fit a child of approximately 6 years old. In our pattern instructions, instead of stipulating row by row to the fair-isle design, we suggest you follow the chart on page 96. This is extremely simple to do—just remember that each square equals 1 stitch, and each horizontal row of square, 1 row. Then just work in stocking stitch following the pattern.

MEASUREMENTS
Completed length (including ribbing) : 6½(7, 7½) inches.
Completed width across Back : 3¼ inches.

TENSION
7 sts and 8½rs. to 1 inch, knitting S.S. on No. 10 Ns.

YOU WILL NEED
1 50grm. Double Knitting
  Wool ball in main colour
  (BLACK)
1 50grm. Double Knitting
  Wool ball in first contrast
  colour (RED)
1 50grm. Double Knitting
  Wool ball in second
  contrast colour (WHITE)
A pair of No. 10 and No. 12
  knitting needles
A crochet hook size 2.50.

BACKS (2 pieces alike):
Using Red wool and No. 12 Ns. cast on 20 sts. Work 2 inches of K.1, P.1 rib. Change to Black wool and No. 10 Ns. Work in S.S. beginning with a K.r, *K.5 sts. Inc. into next st.* Repeat from * to * twice more (23 sts) altogether.
Continuing in S.S., K.1 (3, 5) rs. Begin working fair-isle (see introduction) from chart, and K.24 (26, 28) rs., ending with a P.r.

SHAPE TOP:
Still following fair-isle chart at the same time dec. 1st. at both ends of next r. P.1 r. Dec. 1 st. at both ends of the next 4 rs. Cast off 2 sts. at the beginning of the next 2 rs. Cast off the remaining 7 sts.

PALMS (2 pieces alike):
Using Red wool and No. 12 Ns. cast on 16 sts. Work 2 inches of K.1, P.1 rib. Change to Black wool and No. 10 Ns. Beginning with a K.r, *K.4 sts. Inc. into next st.* Repeat from * to * twice more. K.4 sts. (19 sts.). Continuing in S.S., K.25 (29, 33) more rs, ending with a P.r.

SHAPE TOP:
Dec. 1st. at both ends of next and every following K.r, 5 times altogether. Dec. 1 st. at both ends of next r. Cast off remaining 7 sts.

THUMBS (4 pieces):
FRONTS (2 pieces alike): Using Black wool and No. 10 Ns., cast on 2 sts. Working in S.S., K.1 r. Inc. 1 st. at the end of the next and every following P.r, 5 times (7 sts.). Work 7(9, 11) rs. Dec. 1 st. at both ends of the next 2 rs. P.1 r. Dec. 1 st. at beginning of the next r. Cast off remaining 2 sts.

BACKS (2 pieces alike): Work as for Fronts, but reverse shaping by beginning with a P.r, and then read K. for P. and vice versa.

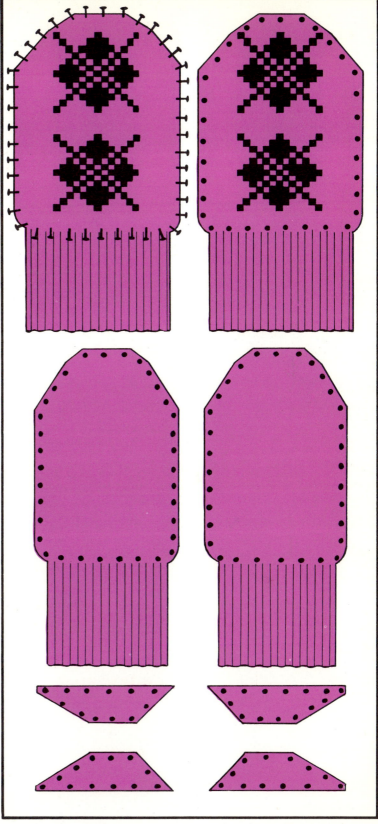

Above are all knitted pieces that make up the mittens. Black dots indicate places for pinning them out.

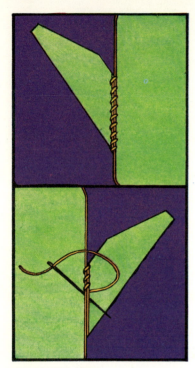

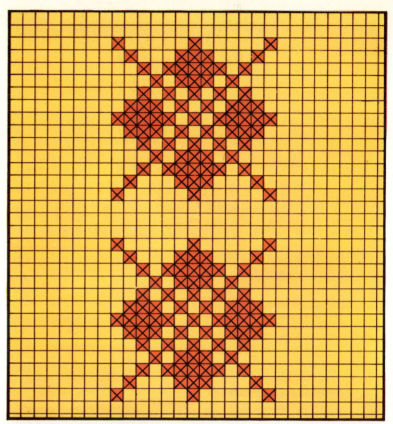

TO MAKE UP

Pin out each piece to size and press as given in Notes. Sew diagonally shaped end of each Thumb piece to appropriate Back and Palm, with lower edge approximately $\frac{3}{4}$ in. above top of ribbing.

Place each Back and Palm together, and using Red wool and a 2.50 crochet hook, join the pieces together by working 1 r. of double crochet sts. all round. Give a final light press.

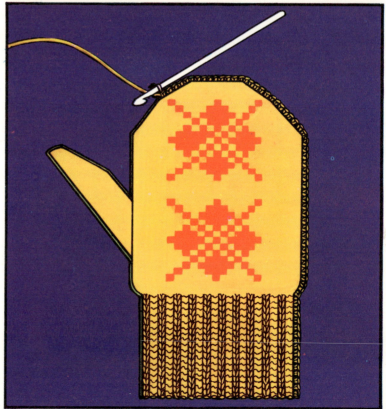